Women & Recovery:
Sex, Sobriety, & Stepping Up

Women & Recovery:
Sex, Sobriety, & Stepping Up

Practical Suggestions for Quality Living in Recovery

ANN D. CLARK, PHD

iUniverse, Inc.
Bloomington

Women & Recovery: Sex, Sobriety, & Stepping Up
Practical Suggestions for Quality Living in Recovery

iUniverse books may be ordered through booksellers or by contacting:

iUniverse
1663 Liberty Drive
Bloomington, IN 47403
www.iuniverse.com
1-800-Authors (1-800-288-4677)

Because of the dynamic nature of the Internet, any web addresses or links contained in this book may have changed since publication and may no longer be valid. The views expressed in this work are solely those of the author and do not necessarily reflect the views of the publisher, and the publisher hereby disclaims any responsibility for them.

Any people depicted in stock imagery provided by Thinkstock are models, and such images are being used for illustrative purposes only.
Certain stock imagery © Thinkstock.

ISBN: 978-1-4759-7282-5 (sc)
ISBN: 978-1-4759-7284-9 (hc)
ISBN: 978-1-4759-7283-2 (ebk)

Library of Congress Control Number: 2013901864

Printed in the United States of America

iUniverse rev. date: 02/04/2013

CONTENTS

I

ABOUT THE AUTHOR

As CEO of ACI Specialty Benefits, Dr. Ann D. Clark leads ACI's strategic planning and direction while actively participating in the community and the media. ACI is ranked in the nation's *Top Ten* of Employee Assistance Programs. ACI's benefits products, including CORE Wellness, SOAR Student Assistance, Leverage Concierge and Affinity Work/Life have consistently led the field in quality, creativity, awards, and recognition. Dr. Clark is nationally known for her expertise in substance abuse and cost containment in the workplace.

Dr. Clark's extensive published works include Citadel Press' best-seller *Surviving Your Boss*, helping employees deal with work/life stress, emotional wellness and ongoing challenges on the job and at home. A popular author for Hazelden Publishing, her works related to recovery include *Alone but Not Lonely; Looking Good: Illusion and Reality; Surrender to Win; Single Parent Families;* and *Anger Management: Get Real!*

Dr. Clark writes from the dual perspectives of her own recovery as well as that of professional training and experience. She holds a doctorate in Psychology from the University of Wisconsin and is a licensed Marriage, Family and Child Therapist. A recipient of numerous awards, Dr. Clark's accolades include: San Diego's "Women Who Mean Business" from the San Diego Business Journal; the "Bravo" award for excellence from the National Association of Women Business Owners; "Outstanding Contribution," Red Cross of Wisconsin; and "Volunteer of the Year," United Way. She remains active in the recovery community, including her role in the film "Differences." Dr. Clark has served on the President's Committee on Mental Retardation.

ACI received special recognition from the National Society for Corporate Communication Betterment for materials developed during the 9/11 crisis and the first year anniversary. Under her leadership ACI was recently named "San Diego's Healthiest Company" by the San Diego Business Journal. She was nominated for San Diego's "Best Boss," and is a frequent presenter for community events.

Dr. Clark is a best-selling author, accomplished motivational speaker, lecturer, and commentator who has appeared on *The Oprah Winfrey Show* and the nationally syndicated *Donahue* shows. Widely published, her articles have appeared in *Glamour*, *Men's Health*, *Redbook* and various other national magazines, as well as newspapers and professional journals.

As a recovering alcoholic, Dr. Clark has been a self-termed "occupational geographic," in which she left university teaching to sell golf clubs. Says Dr. Clark, *"I blamed stress and the pressures of teaching for my problems with addiction. I looked outside of myself for answers. In reading the book* What Color is Your Parachute? *I was struck by the advice to 'ask your friends what you'd be good at.' I followed this advice and my friends told me I would be good at sales. I began to picture myself as a real estate agent or a car saleswoman. It was not a fit. But*

I played golf, and in a friendly game, I learned of an opening at the La Jolla Country Club. I was hired." Thus entering the world of sales, she was able to combine her business experience with her training as a psychologist to develop a new career in employee assistance.

ACI was founded by Dr. Clark in 1983. The company has grown to a position of national prominence and is expanding its international reach, exceeding all expectations. Dr. Clark looks forward to her next book, near completion, addressing expatriates as part of the global workforce. For more information or to contact her directly, visit www.acispecialtybenefits.com or email drann@acispecialtybenefits.com.

II

ACKNOWLEDGMENTS

Special thanks to my dear executive assistant, Genevieve Almodovar, who tirelessly read and reread the manuscript, kept me focused to the completion, the publishing on track and who was inspirational on a daily basis.

I also wish to express gratitude to graphics designer, Aaron Grisafi, who created the beautiful cover for this book and whose work continues to exceed expectations.

Appreciation to copyeditor and writer, Rebecca Ann Jordan, whose fine eye for the details of editing and proofing the manuscript in the final days of creation were and are invaluable.

Finally, a special thank-you to Adora Horton whose energy and enthusiasm inspires me every day.

III

INTRODUCTION

Recovery is a lot like playing a video game—one minute we're in control, and the next minute we feel pursued, victimized, confused, and lost. The words in this book address that jumble of feelings, with suggestions to make the process of recovery easier, faster, and more understandable.

I began my writing career in recovery with the 4th Step. Like Susan Mayer and Gabrielle Solis of *Desperate Housewives*, I started with 13 pages of sex and adventures, ending with a secret . . . that one deeply buried event of my life that I was carrying to the grave. With the self-help of a 12-step program and the loving wisdom of my first sponsor, my life and my writing have progressed. The journey into recovered living and self-knowledge is the purpose for this collection of experiences—my own and others'—and suggestions to make that journey smoother and more enduring for you and those you love.

Whether you are dependent on relationships, food, drama, drugs, alcohol, or the alcoholic, this book can help. One does not have to be a product of an alcoholic home to experience the pain of a dysfunctional family. One does not have to have used drugs to experience the pain of withdrawal—sugar, food, relationships, or even caffeine will do. This book is for anyone who seeks to improve their quality of life, who seeks a lasting and significant relationship, who is looking for practical suggestions and specific techniques that work. This book is for you.

I reference the 12 Steps often throughout the book. The 12 Steps, originated by Alcoholics Anonymous (AA), are the spiritual foundation for personal recovery from the effects of alcoholism, not only for the alcoholic, but also for their friends and family in Al-Anon family groups. Many members of 12-step recovery programs have found that these steps not only provided guidance to stop drinking, but that they became a guide toward a new way of living.

The original 12 Steps published by AA are:

1. We admitted we were powerless over alcohol—that our lives had become unmanageable.
2. Came to believe that a power greater than ourselves could restore us to sanity.
3. Made a decision to turn our will and our lives over to the care of God as we understood Him.
4. Made a searching and fearless moral inventory of ourselves.
5. Admitted to God, to ourselves, and to another human being the exact nature of our wrongs.
6. Were entirely ready to have God remove all these defects of character.
7. Humbly asked Him to remove our shortcomings.
8. Made a list of all persons we had harmed, and became willing to make amends to them all.

9. Made direct amends to such people wherever possible, except when to do so would injure them or others.

10. Continued to take personal inventory, and when we were wrong, promptly admitted it.

11. Sought through prayer and meditation to improve our conscious contact with God as we understood Him, praying only for knowledge of His will for us and the power to carry that out.

12. Having had a spiritual awakening as the result of these steps, we tried to carry this message to alcoholics, and to practice these principles in all our affairs. (Alcoholics Anonymous World Services 1991)

1

RELATIONSHIPS AND EMOTIONS: SEX IS A SLIPPERY PLACE

"Candy is dandy, but liquor is quicker," quipped humorist Ogden Nash, summarizing an age-old view of the relationship between alcohol and sex. Our own experience and common sense tells us that alcohol affects sexual behavior. Whether used by the awkward Seth from *Superbad* to lower his inhibitions in order to finally "get it in" with Jules, or the timid Evan to bolster courage, alcohol is associated with sexual activity in a variety of ways. Sex in sobriety represents a potentially slippery place for women. The newly recovering person, and many "old-timers," may find that sex and dating are uncomfortable without the ease of alcohol and drugs—social lubricants that bolster confidence, lower inhibitions, and mask feelings.

A newcomer recovering from alcoholism, Monica D. points out this dilemma: "I'm really confused. I used to be a party girl. I was popular and dated a lot. I'm divorced now, but I had no trouble when I was single and dating my husband. Now that I'm about six months sober I'm awkward around men. I'm afraid of what they'll think of me. I don't know what to say and I act shy (which I'm not). Also, I don't seem to desire sex. What can I do? I don't want to drink again."

To better understand the relationship of sexual activity and addiction, let's look at what the process actually does. Alcohol or any drug, including food, affects the brain to lower inhibitions and enable people to act in ways which may be contrary to their value systems. In a survey of 3000 women aged 18-50, four out of 10 had been drinking when they slept with their partner for the first time. A whopping 75 percent liked to drink before getting into bed with their husband or boyfriend. More than 50 percent claimed drinking was "part of the dating process" and 14 percent said they can't sleep with their partner without a couple glasses of wine (Herald Sun 2009). Thus, we can see that alcohol and drugs are closely connected to most women's sexual experiences.

Alcohol-related sexual dysfunction presents further complications. For both men and women, alcohol affects orgasmic intensity and overall satisfaction and pleasure. In men who abuse alcohol, testosterone levels are reduced, and impotency may be an immediate side effect. The problems may continue in sobriety. Both sexes have said they have a lack of sexual desire in early recovery (University of Illinois).

Moreover, sexual abuse is present in the histories of recovering women in much higher numbers than in the normal population. Research shows women who were physically or sexually abused as children have a higher likelihood of having drinking problems, and women with a family history of alcoholism are more likely to abuse alcohol than men ("Women & Alcohol").

While sexual issues and abusive experiences may present significant obstacles in the early stages of recovery, the good news is most sexual functions return very quickly. Psychological progress and spiritual awakening occur more slowly. While singles may find this simply inconvenient and frustrating, a difficult problem is presented for marrieds who have a history of sexual performance (or non-performance) as well as expectations of a partner.

Understanding and information will help recovery. There is no doubt that early recovery is a time of confusion and emotional instability. The greatest sexual changes are reported as happening in the first three months. This is consistent with the wisdom of AA, which suggests that new relationships should be avoided in the first year of recovery.

While individual reactions may vary greatly (age, hormone levels, history, support systems, and consumption patterns are factors), it may be helpful to view problems of sexual dysfunction in early sobriety as part of the mainstream experience. Impotency in men, lack of desire in both sexes, fear, and discomfort may be common in early recovery. They are also good reasons for the novice in recovery to abstain from sexual activities during the first phase of sobriety. The associated problems—lack of self-esteem and insecurity—may obscure early recovery goals. Focusing on sexual relationships will further cloud the issues of staying clean and sober, including other forms of abstinence.

It is important for the newcomer to accept that sexual performance is not a primary objective at this time. In the struggle for self-esteem and dignity, the recovering woman can give herself permission to take sexual control of her life and body. Accepting that the body not only needs time to recover from the physiological effects of substance abuse, but must also rebuild sexual functioning, may remove some of the guilt, anxiety and tension around sex in sobriety. Here are some suggestions which may be helpful:

- Seek out same-sex meetings and share your concerns. Be open and honest with your sponsors. Ask about their experience.
- Include sexual experiences in Steps 4 and 5, or do a sexual 4th.
- Consider celibacy for the early phase of sobriety. Avoid new relationships for at least 90 days.
- Communicate openly and frankly to your partner (if you have one) about your needs and feelings.
- Learn more about your body. Many easy-to-read and informative books are found on the internet in abundance.
- Don't hesitate to seek professional help. Ask other recovering individuals to refer you to a therapist or specialized support group.
- Finally, write about it—the experience will be cathartic, and may be the start of your own book.

2

MEN SUFFER TOO

Both physiological and emotional problems affect sexual relationships in the early months of sobriety. Some important factors included alcohol as a social lubricant; beliefs that alcohol and drugs may seem to enhance sexual desire and enjoyment; sexual dysfunction as a result of alcohol abuse, including impotency and loss of desire; and sexual abuse—an important part of many women's histories. Men are often confused in early recovery also.

Eddie, recovering from both drug and alcohol abuse, says, "I really learn a lot from listening to women. I guess now that I am over a year sober, I know that I have been afraid of women, and often was abusive to them because of that fear. My mother was an alcoholic and pretty abusive to me and my brothers. I guess I thought all women had that potential. Sex was about the best thing women had to offer. I guess that sounds awful to a woman, but I'm glad that changed in sobriety. I'm just learning how to date and really talk to women. Sex is a little frightening without warming up with a few drinks, but when my sponsor suggested holding off for a few months, I was relieved. I don't like the word celibacy, but I guess that has helped me a lot in relaxing and getting more comfortable with women."

Like many other men, Eddie associated dating and sex with alcohol. His dysfunctional childhood experiences affected his adult relationships. He is learning, perhaps for the first time, that he can become intimate without the fear of his mother's abusive behavior subconsciously affecting him. He is also learning that alcohol did not make relationships and intimacy easier, but rather made him act in ways that prevented real intimacy.

Rosa speaks of sexual confusion as a distraction from building the foundations of early recovery; "I learned that I wasn't just compulsive about alcohol, but about anything that stopped me from feeling. I found I was very attractive to a lot of men in the program, and did not understand "13-stepping," [a term referring to dating newcomers]. I was very vulnerable and lonely. I confused their sexual interest in me with genuine caring and I stopped listening in the meetings. I was almost as compulsive in sexual areas as I had been in drinking. Luckily, I got a great woman to be my sponsor and she helped me see that recovery comes first."

Maria J., a compulsive overeater, says, "It seems like all my life men had disappointed me. My father had deserted us when I was very young, but I remember being very loyal to him. I began to think all men would abandon me like he did . . . I was really amazed at how fears of abandonment and sexual issues were related. I think many of us use sex to prove we're not rejected."

Women often discover that early sexual relationships can cause both slips and possibly help. Rosa goes on about her early sexual experience in sobriety; "I felt so low and unworthy that his interest in me seemed the only reason to stay sober. I knew I wasn't supposed to get in a relationship so quickly, but it did so much for my self-esteem."

Janet S. said, "I really found the idea of celibacy was very helpful. I'd been having some real up and down feelings about sex—one minute thinking about desire, and the next minute wondering if I would ever want sex again. My sponsor said that these feelings were normal. I decided to abstain from sex in my first year and try dating—something I had never experienced as a teenager. It was great."

Here's a comment from Elizabeth T. who practices both an Al-Anon and AA program: "I think we should read the *Big Book* on this topic. It talks a lot about motives and motivation. Here's a part I like: 'We tried to shape a sane idea for our future sex life. We subjected the relationship to this test: Was it selfish or noble? We asked God to mold our ideals and help us to live up to them. We remembered always that our sex powers were God-given and therefore good, neither to be used lightly or selfishly, nor to be despised and loathed.'"

If you are interested in reading more about this topic, the *Big Book*, Alcoholics Anonymous, and *As Bill Sees It* (with five sections on sex) are excellent sources.

3

Love? Of Course: Self-Love

Serena, recently divorced and six months sober, lives in a recovery home. She has little privacy and feels anxious much of the time. She is fearful of involvement with men, although she misses the physical closeness she had with her ex-husband. She is afraid to date again—at 46 she doesn't know how, but feels a need for sex. She has considered masturbation, but her religious training told her this was immoral and abnormal. She wonders why she can't control her feelings.

Joanie, at 23, is only 17 days sober. She has a boyfriend who is very supportive. They've had a good sexual relationship, but recently, since getting sober, she's felt a loss of desire. She heard some women in a closed meeting talking about vibrators and using them with their partners. Joanie's never even seen one. She's wondering if something's wrong with her. This whole sex thing seems to be changing.

Natalie, very experienced with men, even casually in her drinking and using days, feels comfortable with her own sexuality. Sober six years, at 36 she finds her dates are limited by her own selectivity and higher standards. She wonders if masturbation might enhance her feelings of being okay without a man in her life. But it seems a little too self-contained; what if she gets so completely satisfied she doesn't ever want a man again?

These scenarios were prompted recently when I was asked to speak to a group of recovering women ranging in sobriety from a few days to four years. The topic at their recovery home was "Sex and Early Recovery." I immediately thought back to my own early days of sobriety. Though very shaky and ill, I immediately noticed at my first recovery meeting the number of good-looking men. I thought to myself, "Where were these guys when I was in the bars?" But as time passed and "13-stepping" became part of my own experience, I listened to advice from other women: "Men will pinch your ass, but women will save it."

In early sobriety, dating, relationships and sexual experiences represent potential danger—or slippery places. There is talk about celibacy, no relationships in the first year, dating in or out of the program, and much more. Whatever opinion you share, as a woman, sex was often associated with negative experience.

Frequently, women have little sexual education, are often ill-informed about their own anatomy and physiology, and certainly are not ready to move into relationships in the shaky and confusing days of early sobriety.

Self-love includes masturbation. Almost no sexual issue is without controversy. Certainly masturbation is fraught with misconceptions, guilt-ridden attitudes, misunderstandings and fears. Nothing is more normal or natural than touching oneself for pleasure. Babies do this when they play with their toes. Men do this by stroking a beard or mustache. Sometimes we touch ourselves in a painful way—pinching ourselves to stay awake, or biting our lips to avoid saying something we'll regret. These are all ways of stimulating ourselves.

Masturbation, self-stimulation of the genital or arousal areas (erogenous zones), becomes part of the first orgasmic experience for most young adults, usually in early adolescence. Nearly all men and the majority of women masturbate during adolescence. Again, this is very normal and natural. It becomes a way of learning about sexual gratification before a young person is ready for the intimacy and experience of a sexual partner. In fact, it was reported over 80 percent "really enjoy masturbating" and over 90 percent don't feel guilty about it afterward (Vogels 2010).

This same phase, I think, is important in early sobriety. Most women, and many men, have had numerous negative sexual experiences prior to entering recovery. Studies report as high as 75 percent of women entering inpatient treatment and a high percentage of recovering women in general have been sexually abused; an estimated 70 to 80 percent of men's and women's first sexual experience involved alcohol.

So, relearning about sex, experiencing a period of sexual gratification without emotional and physical involvement with a partner may be an important part of that solid foundation upon which our recovery should be built.

Unfortunately, too many people grow up learning that masturbation is not okay. That it is not normal, not natural. Whether in the form of jokes, or the very real stigmas and punishments imposed by churches, authorities, and parents, society participates in creating guilt, shame, secrecy, and fear around this simple and natural practice. The recovering person, likely to come from a dysfunctional family, is a ready candidate for guilt and shame, and needs special re-education in this area.

Why do we masturbate? The answer is simple. It feels good. It is often comforting in loneliness, meets physiological needs and provides a release of sexual tension. Masturbation is a good stress reducer. It is a harmless physical pleasure. Why is it important in early sobriety? For women especially, the emotional highs and lows of early sobriety may be confused with feelings of loneliness. Too often relationships have formed a barrier against being alone, self-reliance, getting to know oneself, getting to know other women. There are many reasons both women and men get into relationships which are not good choices.

Masturbation provides a sexual release, an experiment with pleasure that, for many women, has previously only been associated with sex with a partner. Perhaps an even more important reason is getting to know your own body, taking care of that body and pampering it.

Taking care of all of ourselves—our spiritual growth, physical health, friendships, family and program of sobriety—includes taking care of physical and sexual needs. Bodies need stimulation. We need to feel loved, including feeling loved by ourselves.

I repeat some advice from the *Big Book*: "We all have sex problems. We'd hardly be human if we didn't. What can we do about them? We reviewed our own conduct . . . were we at fault and what should we have done instead? In this way we tried to shape a sane and sound ideal for our future sex life. We remember always that our sex powers were God-given and therefore good, neither to be used lightly or selfishly, nor to be despised and loathed . . . the right answer will come, if we want it" (Big Book 2012).

Am I dating myself when I reminisce that sex used to be fun? I'm talking about the days b.p. (before the pill) with the Russian-roulette of pregnancy and the steamy, hours-long make-out sessions in the back seat (talk about aerobics). Remember when virginity was a tradable commodity? I even remember when garter belts were necessary—not an erotic invention of *Victoria's Secret*.

Reading the article titles in just one leading women's fashion magazine, I found: "Sex-shy" (why we're still squeamish about sex), "He's Late and I'll Never Meet Another Man" (about catastrophic worrying), "No Regrets Ultimatum" (how to force the male to make commitments), and "Him? Worry About His Body?" (about the male-only problems of love handles, bum butts, penis size and mayonnaise legs).

Men and women seem to start with a desire for the same thing—intimacy of contact. The stereotypes of women just wanting to be held, and the men just wanting to achieve orgasm both seem to be unfounded. Similarly, it is not men who "always" want sex—women want more and more often.

As a society, we think men are the ones that are sex-driven. In an online survey, over 1500 women responded to answer questions about their sexual behavior. About three-quarters of the women said they "like to have sex once a day" (Vogels 2012).

When sex is not fun, what has gone wrong? The differing expectations just outlined are part of an explanation. For alcoholics and addicts, sexual difficulties and dysfunction may well be related to control. Of attempting to control others, the *Big Book* states very strongly, "That was our dilemma." An area of power and control in any relationship is the bedroom.

Family history is another source for problems. Early experiences which fail to provide models of love, trust, the demonstration of affection, or the sharing of feelings, may stand in the way of our demonstrating the positive vulnerability that goes along with a good sexual relationship.

Deeply rooted cultural and family messages can sabotage intimacy and sexual involvement. Unacknowledged guilt and shame haunt relationships in recovery. Both women and men may be afflicted with guilt around sexual acts.

Further, sexual histories for both men and women are important. That women are sexually abused, victims of a range of deviant sexual acts from rape to marital subjugation, is not news. Men, too, have histories of poor sexual experiences which may include abuse or certainly include humiliating sexual experiences in conflict with their personal value systems. Both partners bring the ghosts of family and sexual history to new relationships.

The joy of a healthy sexual relationship is part of the promise of sober living. In spite of the many real concerns about casual sex, sex is still an important part of life, a way of communicating love and creating special bonds. Putting the fun into, or back into, sexual experiences involves coming to grips with personal issues which inhibit trust and intimacy. Breaking old patterns is crucial for sexual recovery.

Sometimes professional help is needed. It is not necessary to start with a sex therapist. A very valuable and excellent resource, sex therapy may really be a later step, focusing on problems of physical and symptomatic dysfunction. Exploring issues of family origin, communicating, trusting, flirting, and improving dating skills may be a better first step. Often simply talking to another recovering person (sponsor and friends), may be a place to start. Learning what is normal in recovery may be different from what we expected. The experience of others helps us understand what we are going through. Perhaps we're not that unique after all.

Good relationships take work, time and commitment. Skill and technique are also necessary. And with all the tribulations, there can be tremendous rewards for the effort. For me, living a complete and balanced life in sobriety includes fun. And sex? Definitely.

It's no wonder we feel the pressures of being in a relationship. Certainly the holiday season reminds us that much of the world has chosen to exist as couples. I notice on every holiday from Easter to Ground Hog Day, couples come out of the woodwork. Did everyone resolve their control and intimacy issues when I wasn't looking? What ever happened to the eternal searching on *Sex in the City?*

Let's talk about the non-couple. The woman who doesn't have a man. And the woman who doesn't want one. And the woman who doesn't want the one she has. And so forth. The same categories exist for men.

Says Andrea G., "I've just ended a relationship that began like the happy ending of a cheesy romance novel. He had pursued me with romantic words and passionate embraces. We both loved frozen Milky Ways. So what happened? Was it his 'Tofu Surprise' that first night he made dinner that turned me off? Did my insistence on his lowering the toilet seat take the edge off romance? Or was it simply two people whose issues with intimacy, trust, and control seemed more important than being happy? Well, the answer is probably not simple.

"But," she continues, "the bottom line here is that I'm once again forcing myself to sleep in the middle of my queen-size bed, throw away all the saccharin greeting cards taped to my bathroom mirror, and control the impulse to call his answering machine with a list of his character defects."

Now, if you've got it made with your partner, stop reading here. But if you're feeling a little lonely and alone, here are some tips on how to beat the love drought—how to take advantage of being somebody when nobody loves you. How to capture the excitement and freedom you can have being a complete and whole non-couple.

- Make positive resolutions: Now's the time to sign up for "Dirty Dancing" or Chinese cooking lessons. Commit yourself to positive action and affirmations around new learning: writing poetry, journaling, reading about dream interpretation, or perhaps acquiring a new job-related skill to further your knowledge in your career.

- Be confident of your sexual allure: Too often the loss of a partner makes us feel unattractive. Remember, just as the 5th Step provides a solid foundation for your program, sexy underwear does it for your confidence. Wear your prettiest, sexiest "undies" or dress up today. Flirt outrageously for the fun of it. Experiment with a new lip gloss, or ask a friend to trade pedicures. Smile at the postman or a stranger in the grocery line.

- Hit the telephone: Call everyone on your 12-step program phone list. Leave messages just to say hello and keep in touch. Tell the truth. If you've neglected friends for passion, make amends and start over—especially with your women friends. They'll understand.

- Do a four-step inventory on the relationship: In writing, (and honestly) take a look at what you contributed to the break-up. Not who-left-whom, or the "reverse vanity" of being too hard on yourself. Just a simple, written 4th Step, followed by the 5th, then Steps 6 and 7 to focus on improving your skill in relationships, communication, building intimacy, etc. Again, let the experience serve you. Help yourself to be better in all your relationships by inventorying this one.

- Examine expectations: In your inventory, consider the possibility that you may have unrealistic expectations of what your mate or lover should be. Was Mr. Wrong not Mr. Right because of real or perceived difficulties? Was the fear of losing your autonomy (read: control) part of the problem? Did you expect too much of him—and yourself—in the early stages, before intimacy and trust were really established?

- Don't eat: Resist the temptation to fill empty hours or an empty bed with food. Nothing will make you feel more confident, sexy and secure than looking good.

- Avoid weddings, love songs, and romantic movies: Even if you ended the relationship, you may find a void in your life. Stay positive and out of slippery places. I personally don't listen to lyrics like "Wasting Away Again in Margaritaville" anymore. So, I also don't want to hear, "Someday He'll Come Along" or, "How Can I Go on Without You." Switch your station to the funky, "How Ya Like Me Now."

- Take the initiative: There are many good ideas for pursuing romance in this and any other month. Take the initiative by inviting a small group, including Mr. Possibly, to a play. Invite new people, male and female, out for coffee. Let friends know you're available for activities. Offer to babysit. Go to new and different 12-step meetings. Don't sit around waiting for Prince Charming to knock on your apartment door looking for directions to the ball.

What about love in early or at any stage of recovery? My own experience is not uncommon. I found that as I became physically sober, I was motivated to get on with my life. Falling in love seemed a logical next step. But at that point in time what I really wanted was affection and warmth. Did I even know what that romantic and overused word meant?

Love is certainly a universal experience; yet while it is so common, it remains a baffling condition to most human beings. Certainly those of us who are recovering are no exception.

We ask ourselves: What is love? How do I give and receive love? Do I have the capacity for love? Why do I fall in and out of love? Do we have to be romantic and unrealistic about love? Does love change as we change? Is love different now that I am sober?

What is love? Let's examine what authorities say. Leo Buscaglia is sure that "Love is active, not passive. It is continually engaged in the process of opening new doors and windows so that fresh ideas and questions can be admitted" (Buscaglia 2004).

Love/luv (n.)

1. A strong feeling of affection and concern toward another person, as that arising from kinship or close friendship.
2. A strong feeling of affection and concern for another person accompanied by sexual attraction. (Amercican Heritage Dictionary 2011)

Erich Fromm, author of the classic *The Art of Loving,* also describes love as an active agent: "Love is an activity, not a passive affect; it is a 'standing in,' not a 'falling for.' In the most general way, the active character of love can be described by stating that love is primarily giving, not receiving."

Fromm goes on: "Mature love is a union under the condition of preserving one's integrity, one's individuality. Love is an active power . . . In love this paradox occurs that two beings become one and yet remain two" (Fromm 2006).

Research shows that lack of love may cause illness and even death. Abraham Maslow says that love is an inherent human need, absolutely necessary in order for us to become all that we are capable of becoming. The lack of love in infants creates mental retardation and physical problems, and if the infant is severely deprived, it will die due to lack of love. Clearly, we have a lifelong human need for love that must be met, just like our need for food, air, or shelter ("Abraham Maslow").

You may be thinking, "Sure, I need to love and be loved, but is it really worth it?" Underlying that question is another question, "Can I survive without it? Because the risk of rejection terrifies me. Are the rewards of making myself vulnerable really as great as the risk?"

I think the answer is yes. M. Hodge insists in *Your Fear of Love* that "We can discover for ourselves that it is worth the risk to love, even though we tremble and even though we know we will sometimes experience the hurt we fear" (Hodge 1967). Dr. Gerald Jampolsky is equally encouraging; "Let us continue to be involved in a process of personal transformation in which we are only concerned about giving and not about getting" (Jampolsky 2010).

In sobriety, it may be necessary to examine how we have learned, or have not learned, to love. Certainly sobriety and the start of a new year provide many opportunities for reflection on loving relationships. Step 8 suggests that we examine the basis for our relations with others. All too often love was confused with co-dependency, remorse, guilt, or the need for drinking, or enabling a partner. A good start for examining love in a sober life is to begin with the wisdom of Bill W. In *As Bill Sees It: The AA Way of Life* there are 13 indexed references to love.

In the spirit of new beginnings it may be helpful to pick one theme that all authors stress—giving as a critical part of loving. Bill W. says, "Always one must ask, 'What is the best and most loving thing I can do?'" (W. 1967). Perhaps now is the time for you to answer that question.

- Start with a dictionary definition of love and then develop your own. Here are some ideas: love includes a strong physical attraction, common interests and shared goals. Are these a part of your definition?

- Similarly, define romance. Is it different from love? Is it required for love? Was romance or lust tied to alcohol and drug use in your own history? Remember, even the most glamorous single glass of champagne is still alcohol.

- What do you want in a loving relationship? Be specific. Can he smoke? Wear V necks? What feelings do you want to experience with him? Is anger okay? How much? Make a long list. These are not criterion, but a way of clarifying your thoughts.

- Finally, remember that love isn't exclusively tall, dark, and handsome. Love comes in the form of people listening to others, people helping others, people who are willing to give before receiving. Your 12-step program is the ideal way to experience love. Renewing your spiritual commitments can be the best way to build a new relationship with your higher power. Love doesn't have to come in pairs. Act lovingly to yourself and others. Remember, you are one of kind and with credentials like that, Cupid's bound to be aiming at you.

4

Sober Fun:
A Contradiction in Terms?

Because I was a "party girl," I couldn't envision fun without alcohol and drugs. In my life, before alcoholism brought me to my knees, the social life I enjoyed seemed very normal—parties at home (with a near-lethal punch), football brunches on crisp fall days, with a few Bud Lights to start, and trendy dinner parties with three wine courses.

Is sobriety a sentence to a life of boredom? Not according to the women I know. My own experience is that life has never been more exciting and more fun. Sober women share some of their ideas for sober fun.

Margo C. explains her definition, "I am 24 years old and have not had a drink in over two years. I firmly believe that a major reason for my continued sobriety is the places I chose to go to for fun.

"I stay out of threatening environments, nightclubs, or wild parties, attending functions that are associated with the 12-step programs in my town and nearby. I attend a lot of outdoor get-togethers and I love attending conventions. It's a great place to meet sober men and new women friends."

Music offers a ton of entertainment and many women enjoy the many events in which alcohol is not served, or is not pushed and they are still able to have a good time. Dianna, an avid dancer, and lover of music, almost lost this activity when drinking. "I couldn't bear to listen to music. It seemed every single song I loved brought back painful memories. So I kept the "loboto-box" going. I used TV to anesthetize what was left of my feelings."

Marilyn S., a nurse, is not recovering, but likes to go dancing to have a good time. She recommends taking dance classes. Beginners are usually welcome, and partners interchange during the class. Marilyn points out the exercise and meeting new people add value also.

"I like to go to meetings," answered Lorraine B. "I really enjoy the fun, stimulation and special feelings I get from attending 12-step meetings."

"The beach," Georgie, three years sober, responds. "I spent too many days afraid to go out alone. The paranoia and fear I felt from drinking and using caused me to stay inside on sunny days. Now that I'm sober I have a special joy in the sun and sand that I denied myself for so long."

"Believe it or not, it's school for me" replies Sandra M. "I meet terrific guys (and lots of younger ones find me attractive) and lots of great women. I learned about clubs and events, and generally have a lot of fun studying. This may sound weird but I always thought I was stupid. My father felt women shouldn't go to college (he was an alcoholic by the way) and made me feel really dumb. Now I feel proud of myself and know that I'm going to graduate, but not soon. Anyway, I sure recommend the benefits of going back to school, or like me, starting from scratch."

With over 20 years of sobriety, Millie has plenty of experience. She addressed the newcomer, suggesting, "I thought sobriety would be the end of good times. I loved going out and felt doomed when I went to AA. It was really different then—not many women to talk with, no dancing or Al-Anon clubs. But I was told to stay away from slippery places. To me that meant bars, booze, and what the book calls 'lower companions.' I haven't changed that rule very much over the course of my sobriety, and I've still had a whole lot of fun."

Finally, several women mentioned Al-Anon clubs. Most remarked that these are safe places for them. Said Alice D., "You might find some men hitting on you, but that happens everywhere. Just sit with the women and get acquainted. When you're new, the women can show you the way."

During several interviews, I heard many viewing recovery as broadening in perspective. Said Patti S., "I live life now. Everything I do is sober fun now that I have a recovery program. I enjoy work and play, my dogs, and friends. Whether we walk on the beach or rest after a hard day's work—we are loving life."

Having fun is an integral part of recovery. Use the tips these women have provided to help yourself broaden your interests and perspective in sobriety.

5

THE STRUGGLE FOR INTIMACY

What about intimacy? Along with love, this concept is much discussed, blamed, misunderstood, and maligned. Consider current book titles: *The Struggle for Intimacy*; *Do I Have To Give Up To Be Loved By You*; *The Road Less Traveled*; and *Power Games*, to name only a few. The implications are of battle, turmoil, pain, and difficulty. People discuss their "fear of intimacy," a clinical term that is used often to describe alcoholics, addicts, and adult children of addicts and alcoholics. Men are often described in stereotypic terms as lacking the ability to be intimate.

Yet women don't seem to have any greater ease with intimacy than men. Sometimes women's relationships are described as being more intimate than men's friendships, yet many men point to close attachments and deep, trusting relationships with other men.

Credible data are difficult to find when so few people seem able to describe the behavior of intimacy. What then is intimacy? How is it important in sobriety, and what are the special issues that women have around intimacy?

Gate B. shares, "Intimacy prior to sobriety meant sharing in conversation my dreams, feelings, and ideas, but through a filtering process based on satisfying another's expectations and approval of myself. Eight months later I experienced intimacy to the degree that I was willing to share in my 12-step program. Allowing emotions to surface and talking about them to a group gives me an intimate connection far more satisfying than what I thought I experienced with drinking or using pills. Intimacy involves risk because others are at different levels of awareness or understanding. The risk of not sharing could be the excuse I look for to go take that one drink."

Roxanne F. points out that there are no shortcuts; "Many people are looking for intimacy without investing time. I don't think that's possible. Sexual and physical togetherness is, but not intimacy." This is an important concept. Addicts and alcoholics by definition look outside themselves to alter uncomfortable feelings and want a quick fix.

Gate's touching sentiments illustrate her need to please others when she was drinking and using. Getting close or intimate was a way of finding out others' expectations so she could attempt to please them.

Roxanne points out an additional element of the quick payoff. Too often, recovering people want an immediate payoff for their efforts. Intimacy, or being close, includes an element of trust that by definition can be developed only over time.

What is this elusive concept? The dictionary describes intimacy very simply as "close personal relations; a close union." The Latin root of the word means "inmost."

Shirley uses that word in her story: "Sharing my innermost thoughts and feelings with women is something I've learned in sobriety. That's where I think women have to start. Sometimes I didn't even know what I felt. How could I share something I didn't have with anyone, especially a man I wanted to make a good impression on?"

Jane M. speaks, "My idea of intimacy was total oneness. I wanted to spend every moment with my husband, do everything together, and have both of us thinking about each other when we were apart. Now, that sounds awful. And we got a divorce. In sobriety I've learned that my definition of intimacy was really the worst kind of dependency. Women especially have been role models for me to see that I have to bring something to a relationship, and to do this I have to live my own life, find hobbies and interests, and then find a partner to share—not engulf—my life." In this, Jane points out an important characteristic of recovering women as well as Adult Children of Alcoholics/Addicts—trouble setting limits, repacking privacy and boundaries.

Finally, Cella M. talks about a key myth in recovery. She says, "I've heard so often in meetings people think, "If you get to know me, you won't like me." I thought this was true of me. Now I know most of us feel this way. I'm not unique. It seemed to me this was my real trouble with developing close relationships. It's a contradiction to say we have to be open and honest and share our deep feelings, when we think the deep part is unacceptable. Of course, we can't show that, and must conceal and create barriers to intimacy. And the truth is that I'm a loveable, nice person. In sobriety I am learning to show the real me to people and they are accepting me as I am."

Intimacy, like many new behaviors in sobriety, must be practiced, learned and relearned. In order to learn, risks must be taken and mistakes are a part of the learning process. But the rewards to the learning process are exciting. Loving relationships, joyful companionship, understanding, safety, and serenity are only a few of the outcomes of learning to be close, to develop a capacity for intimacy. Start the process now. Sobriety really is a new beginning.

6

OUR EMOTIONS INCLUDE ANGER

"I drank so I wouldn't have to feel." —Sue M.

"Cutting me off on the freeway," "Holding up the line in the grocery store while she counts her pennies," "Using the telephone while I'm sleeping in the morning," "Being late to meet me, again," "Talking down to me in a business meeting where I can't defend myself," "He hit me and I wanted to kill . . ."

Petty irritations, minor differences, felonious assault, and battery—what do these descriptions have in common? They are situations which women spontaneously described when I asked, "What makes you angry?"

In recovery, a major stumbling block for women, and men, is dealing with anger. Previously, I wrote about the effects of anger on the body—A pain in the neck, blowing up, and serious stress reactions which may permanently damage our health. Let's begin with what anger is. What is your definition?

Anger is a form of emotional communication. It is our mind's way of saying, "I don't like what's happening. I'm uncomfortable. Pay attention to me." Our mind uses body signals to attract our attention—primarily adrenaline, which increases the heart rate, slows digestion, causes blood vessels to contract, and pupils to dilate—a generalized stress reaction. But this reaction is not unique to anger; it is similar to eustress or happy-stress reaction, and is very similar to the changes occurring during lust, infatuation, and falling in love.

What makes us label this reaction as anger, then, is our interpretation of events. We have interpreted the circumstances surrounding this reaction as dangerous—something to fear.

The fear associated with anger is usually fear of loss, a perceived threat. That fear can be centered on an abstract loss (loss of prestige, self-esteem, a relationship), or around a specific role, or value (loss of possessions, a job or role, or fear of physical harm). Fear signals us to take action to protect ourselves from this perceived threat or loss.

So far, so good. This sounds very logical—we perceive a threat, feel anger, and take action to protect ourselves. The fact is it's not that simple. Women have a particular problem in the anger cycle, as do many men and children from alcoholic families. Many may find their reactions to anger at the extreme—some never feeling angry, others blowing up over petty wrongs.

What is unique about women and their reactions to anger? Cultural and family training particularly influences women not to show or even feel anger. The angry little girl is an unattractive and unfeminine picture. The "sugar and spice" image is imposed at an early age. Girls and women are taught to calm ruffled feathers, be peacemakers, compromise, keep quiet, be good, and generally learn that approval, and even affection is denied to them when they exhibit fighting, hitting, crying, swearing, tantrums, shouting, or anger.

Angry women are threatening to others. They upset a balance; they destroy a seemingly tranquil situation. They make trouble.

Women learn at an early age to conceal their anger. The next step is to feel guilty, depressed, and unsure of themselves when they feel angry. They begin to doubt that their anger is legitimate. This leads to feeling like a victim—ignored, or discounted, certainly feeling the powerlessness that so plagues alcoholics—and so frequently sends the person looking for acceptable ways to express the anger, ways that are probably labeled passive expression of aggressive feelings.

Denise J. tells us, "I was taught to be a 'Stepford Wife.' Now I know that my drinking kept the anger and resentment hidden. When I got sober (of course, my husband had left me) people commented on how angry I was."

Penny, an active member of Overeaters Anonymous, says, "People told me I was eating to avoid anger—literally stuffing it down. I didn't understand any of that. Now I've learned that I had no words to express anger. All I'd ever seen was my father shouting and drinking and my mother crying and doing whatever he said. What role models?"

Mariette, a recovering cocaine user, shares, "I was very attracted to angry men. The more they shouted, swore, and waved their arms, the better I liked it. I equated anger with strength. Women didn't have either one. It was only in sobriety that I saw the pattern—and my own ways of getting even: being late, headaches, not cleaning, wearing un-attractive outfits, and using drugs."

"If we were to live we had to be free of anger . . . anger is the dubious luxury of normal men and women, but for us alcoholics it is poison." So states the *Big Book of AA*.

"Who wouldn't be angry?" asks Jeanne M. "My husband divorced me because I went into treatment, not because I was drinking. He thought it was a matter of willpower. And now that my head is clear, I think he really used my drinking to keep me dependent on him, doing whatever he wanted. Now I'm broke and have to move my two kids out of their home. He has a girlfriend, who's younger and not an alcoholic. I'm working at a minimum wage job because I quit school to marry him. I hear in the program that we're not supposed to be angry. What a laugh. I'll say it again, who wouldn't be angry?"

This story is a common one; anger and recovery seem to go hand-in-hand. What exactly is anger? The *Big Book* equates it with resentment, which arises because ". . . . our self-esteem, our pocket-books, our ambitions, our personal relationships (including sex) were hurt or threatened." Hurt and threat suggest fear, a well-known underlying component of anger. And indeed, women have reason to be afraid. Since the studies show that the majority of women entering treatment programs have experienced sexual abuse, not to mention the emotional and physical abuse they may have endured, we should not be surprised then to learn that anger is a response common among women.

From a physiological point of view, anger is a state of readiness. The nervous system goes into emergency operation to prepare for action. More sugar pours into our blood so we will have energy to fight or run. Our blood circulates faster; the heart pumps rapidly. Our eyes even dilate so we can see better. But when this danger signal passes, shouldn't we relax, let our bodies return to a normal state? Sure, but we don't.

When anger and resentments keep building, the body stays on alert. This may begin a series of physical reactions which lead to stress-related illness and certainly severe wear and tear on the body and emotional stability.

If you're always tired, consider this—people who are often angry or controlling suppressed rage are in a continual state of muscular tension. It's like controlled drinking. The body is alert to conceal any signs of a problem—the anger can't show. And our bodies feel the pressure; the fatigue is very real.

Many angry people clench their teeth and fists, chew their lips and fingernails; symbolically they guard against angry words getting out. Muscles of the jaw and neck can become overdeveloped. Serious back, neck, and arm pains, apparently of unknown origin, can be symptomatic of the stress of guarding against revealing signs of anger.

"I'm itching to get my hands on him." Yes, anger is related to itching, hives, dermatitis, and even acne. The severe mood swings associated with anger and its concealment, as well as changes in hormone level (on-going in the unique physiology of women) can produce high levels of excess oil, resulting in pimples.

The American Headache Society reports between 30 to 78 percent of the population experience tension headaches (Cox 2010). Unexpressed anger results in tension. Note how language links headaches and repressed anger: "I feel like blowing my stack." "I've got to let off steam." "You're a pain in the neck." "My head is killing me."

Anger headaches are caused by a tightening of the muscles surrounding the skull. They may feel like a band squeezing the head, or a very tight cap or headband. Migraines, the most severe of headaches, affect women three times more than men ("About Migraine").

Gastrointestinal problems may also be clues to swallowing anger. The stomach reacts to this the same way it reacts to other toxins. It hurts. And this pain can turn into ulcers, dietary problems, and chronic pain. Some people swallow anger by swallowing food; the relationship between anger and obesity is a well-established one.

Could this most common of all ailments also be related to anger? Yes, says Cornell Medical School. A group of women and men were exposed to the same cold germs. And, you guessed it, the group that was angry, depressed and frustrated with their personal lives caught the colds.

This brief overview of the relationships of anger to physical health is just a starting point. For newly recovering people whose bodies are already vulnerable, physical illness is a very real concern. Recognition of the how and where we inflict anger on our bodies, as well as the cause, is a good start to learning ways to deal openly and honestly with our anger.

Causes of anger are complex and often deeply buried in both the subconscious and the past. Coping with anger through 12-step programs, especially in the 4th and 5th Steps, is a great start for the person who is committed to a sober life.

Health in sobriety requests that we deal with issues. Everyone has to face dealing with anger. The next obvious question is, "I can relate to what you've said, Ann, but what is the next step?" The answer is there are no quick fixes to a lifetime pattern that suddenly isn't working.

But commitment to change is what recovery is all about. If you want to change habits and patterns, here are some suggestions to explore. You may wish to seek professional help—classes in assertiveness training or working with a professional therapist, for example. Certainly a 12-step approach to dealing with anger and reading the many publications about anger and the recovering person are a few starting points.

The following techniques may be helpful as you learn new ways to express and handle anger:

- Time carefully: Choose the right time to express your anger. Remember H.A.L.T. and don't try to express angry feelings when you or the other person is Hungry, Angry, Lonely, Tired, or short on time.

- State your case: Say how you feel using "I" messages ("I feel as though I'm not being heard"). "Acc-you-sations" such as "You don't care about me" will be perceived as attempts to place blame.

- Give data: Be factual when you're explaining why you're upset. Be specific and current. Don't go back to the past for more ammunition.

- Ask for action: Don't be vague. Let the person know specifically what you want. Use clear, direct language: "When you read the paper, I feel discounted. In the future will you put the paper down when I talk to you?"

- Listen and clarify: Give the other person an opportunity to express their feelings about the situation, and be certain that you understand them before going on. The phrase, "I hear you saying . . ." may help here.

- Agree: Look for a win/win solution. The competitive or win/lose solution won't help. Try saying, "You may be right." Notice I didn't say "You are right."

- Fight fair: Don't hit below the belt. Labeling, name-calling, preaching, threatening, and lecturing are just a few of the tactics that are meant to hurt, not help. And, in this electronic age, don't send an angry text message or voicemail to someone's phone. Remember, you can't take that back.

- Help helps: If you're stuck, get help to deal with anger, or recognize that your response is out of proportion to the situation (hitting, shouting, refusing to communicate). It's likely that "wreckage of the past" is a problem. Help may be found through any of the 12-step programs, sponsorship, the 4th and 5th Steps, and professional therapy. Don't risk—ask for help.

7

WHO, ME?

Self-esteem has become a recovery buzzword. Sobriety yuppies use it liberally—"What, you don't have a BMW? Where's your self-esteem?" Personally, I think self-esteem is related to what's in your wardrobe. Yes, it's the condition of your panties and bras. Are you still saving pantyhose with thigh-high craters to wear under slacks? Do you have bikini briefs older than your sobriety? There's an equivalent for the boys too. I suspected my marriage was in trouble when he switched from baggy boxer shorts to Jockey "Scants."

Self-esteem is an important part of any 12-step recovery program, and certainly is critical for comfortable, sober living. An early reference in the *Big Book* relates to Step 4, dealing with anger and resentments:

"We asked ourselves why we were angry. In most cases it was found that our self-esteem . . . our personal relationships (including sex) were hurt or threatened. So we're sore . . . On our grudge list we set opposite each name our injuries. Was it our self-esteem . . . which had been interfered with?"

Both the *Twelve and Twelve* and the *Big Book* go on to speak of the foundation of sobriety, warning us not to skimp on comment, not to make mortar without sand. Well, if you'll excuse the bad pun and stay lighthearted as you read this, I recommend a self-esteem foundation of silk and lace, making your bed and throwing away old pizza boxes.

How frivolous, you say. Heresy, even. Surely there's more to self-esteem than a shopping spree at *Nordstroms*. Of course there is. But too many women feel how they look on the outside is more important than how they feel on the inside. Too often appearances rather than feelings govern their sense of personal worth—their self-esteem.

What does self-esteem look like? What can we see and measure? Self obviously means you and me. But is it that outside or public-self which may have been verbally and physically abused? Is it that self that sees only defects? Is it the perfectionistic self, so common to the alcoholic/addict, demanding control and setting unrealistic standards? Or is it the "true" self—the child within the adult, the real me? I asked Sue P., a compulsive overeater and alcoholic, about this, and her answer was illuminating:

"It's definitely my public-self that was criticized by my mother. She (an unrecovered Al-Anon) would become cold and judgmental of me. Then I turned to food for warmth. I would feel my 'real self' come out when I ate. A self that was loved and okay. Food, and later alcohol, nurtured me. Today I do that for myself. I know the 'real self' needs love and not food. When I overeat I know my self-worth is lost—that public self my mother didn't value is taking over."

Esteem comes from the Latin word *aestimare* meaning to estimate. We can estimate our value with money, applause, compliments, or diamonds. This is the behavioral or measurable component of self-esteem. But another way to measure value is one which we can't see, hear, feel, or put in the bank. That is how we feel.

Feeing happy or proud, knowing you've done a good job, enjoying the beauty of a sunset, or a balloon flying free—these are measures of value, a very personal measure. Another reader, Helen T., talks about one of these emotional measures: "I just don't have the words to explain this, but I love how I feel when I see someone from AA on the street or in a car. I feel connected—like I'm part of a big secret. I feel really good." This emotional measure of value can help the recovering person measure worth. If we know our actions have value, we don't need an outside measure of worth.

But for the recovering people, especially from dysfunctional homes, the stamp of value may only come from others. For many, our histories of embarrassment and humiliation cause us to measure our self-esteem by what people say about us. We may have no inner feelings of worth. We may only have experienced value when others provided it to us. Let me give you a personal example.

In my own recovery program I have tried to do good deeds. Whether small, like sending an unsigned "You're Special," card to a friend or some larger act, like donating to a philanthropic project, I find I want to tell someone what I have done.

Unlike the "Millionaire" on TV handing out anonymous checks from his armchair, never to be seen by the audience, I crave recognition. I want to call my sponsor, tell my best friend, and have the evening television news acknowledge my "unselfish" contribution.

Where does this begin? Why isn't the act of giving or helping enough for me? Why do I need more? A simple answer is alcoholics always need more. Like all compulsive personalities, we have no concept of enough.

In my family, my alcoholic father only rewarded outcome. He valued As on my report cards, winning in competition, chores completed. Because he could not be affectionate, he dispensed love in the form of money.

There were two messages in this: as an adult, I am what I do. And, I should get something when I'm a good girl. Is it surprising then as an adult I find little intrinsic reward in a good deed? The value of esteem of my actions comes from the recognition of others. I have high "other-esteem," and low self-esteem.

Sober living requires attention. For many recovering people that means creating self-esteem from scratch. So how does any person learn their positive worth? Children from "normal" families learn self-esteem primarily through feeling secure. They have a place in the family which is theirs alone. They are wanted and loved just for being, not doing. Here are some ways to build security in an adult world.

- Create belonging: Become a part of a new family and community. 12-step work is ideal for this. Volunteering and helping others assures your place in a new family. You can recreate an environment that teaches value for being.
- Give up drama: Stop performing for an audience. Are you still a drama queen trying to dress and act to please and impress people who don't exist? Stop worrying about what other people think. Stop exhausting yourself with a value system that doesn't work.
- Pets before people: My cocker spaniel doesn't understand cellulite. He doesn't own a tape measurer or a Retin-A Wrinkle Scanner. Leave it to a pet to teach you unconditional love and make you feel good.
- Follow the admonitions of the *Big Book*: Build a solid foundation for sobriety with "How It Works"—honesty,

open-mindedness, and willingness. Then put the past behind you to move on.

- Finally, clean out your underwear drawer: Wear your fanciest teddy on a gloomy day and your sexiest nightie to bed when you're all alone. Repeat after me, "You're special and I love you."

8

PHYSICAL HEALTH

A column I wrote, "Outwitting the Body: Dieting in Sobriety," was prompted by a question from Mary T. She had begun to eat a lot; she wore a size three sizes larger since giving up alcohol and drugs; "I wonder if I am substituting one addiction for another, but also find that my eating now is different. I seem to be out of control. Is there something I should know about how to diet in sobriety?" Yes, Mary, there are some important differences.

Most people, not just women, want to lose weight. The typical approach is to make a decision to diet, use "Sweet and Nothing" in your coffee, substitute yogurt for ice cream, plan but never execute an exercise program, and skip the cake in birthday meetings. Maybe "skinny powders," increased running, fasting programs, a new diet book, and a 12-step approach to overeating are part of your plan. How do you diet?

Nancy H. says, "I diet in my head. I plan and talk, but the weight stays on. I notice that my eating now follows some of the patterns of my drinking. I snack before going out to dinner, just like I used to drink before I went to parties. I also sneak food even when I'm alone."

A lot of women and men share Nancy's and Mary's problems and concerns. How can we outwit a body that gives us signals defying logic and reason? Education is a place to start.

Here is a fact: your body more than your mind determines your weight and eating patterns. While researchers don't know precisely the mechanism which regulates fitness, there seems to be a "set point." Cells that store fat apparently release chemical signals telling the brain to ask for more. The hypothalamus, working through the unconscious, is a part of this system.

The sight and smell of food can raise the set point. The media, with luscious food ads, promote more fat. Exercise, on the other hand, can lower that set point. Finally, a woman's hormonal balance is constantly changing; women often take for granted these changes and imbalances, responding to chemical signals without thinking.

Our opponent, the set point, is tireless. It is cunning, baffling, and powerful. When we get below the set point, the brain sends out signals that we are hungry. Early sobriety is an emotionally unstable condition for many people. It is common to experience mood swings—emotional highs and lows. This quality is also associated with people who are both obese and overeaters. One researcher suggests that when people eat below their set point, they feel suffering, which sets up a component of rebellion—again, a characteristic of alcoholics and addicts.

At this point, you may be saying, "Yes, all of this is true for me. But I've tried everything. Nothing works for me. What can I do to break this cycle, to outwit my body's signals?"

- Surrender: If the set point theory is valid, and researchers and nutritionists find considerable evidence that it is, diets don't work. Dieting threatens the body, and metabolism slows. Calories are burned more slowly to maintain a plateau near the set point.

- Exercise: Here's another suggestion you may not want to hear. Exercise is the most effective technique in changing metabolic rates, set point function, and rate of calorie burn. Don't be grandiose, however. Begin just for today to walk instead of ride, briskly moving an extra block or a mile. Don't wait for the mood to grab you. You don't need new shoes or matching sweats. Just start.

- Drugs don't work: Coffee and cigarettes (and amphetamines) have an appetite-suppressing effect that is misleading. Actually, they have a significant rebound effect. While one or all acts to turn down the set point, like the volume control on your TV, this only works while you are using the drug. When you quit, the set point returns to normal, often with a rebound effect of weight gain.

- Use what works: Most recovering people find that the 12-step programs work to control substance abuse. Take that same model into your food program. Simple principles such as, "one day at a time," "ask for help," "call your sponsor," etc., may help you control your eating. Get a food sponsor, and practice the program.

- Reexamine your priorities and expectations: Set point theory does not provide quick or easy solutions. It suggests long-term changes, one day at a time, but also a positive solution, a direction of effort, and a way to feel good, and outwit your body. Sobriety is about feeling good.

9

"HERSTRESS"

Stress is related very much to our emotional and physical states in sobriety. To say that women are stress-conscious is an understatement. Certainly, stress is the buzzword of this Information Age. But what information do we actually have about stress? More specifically, what do we know about the unique stressors which affect women? What is "HERstress?"

Stress refers to the chemical, physical, and physiological stimulation which prepares us to respond to perceived threat. The danger does not have to be real. Famous stress researcher, Hans Selye, found that the body's response to bad news, or distress, is the same as eustress, the positive response to good news—excitement, elation, surprise. I would add a third type, HERstress, referring to the continual adaptation required of women due to their unique physiology as well as social and cultural conditioning.

The Female Stress Syndrome, its effects and ways to reduce and control the symptoms, deserves our attention. These are some special stressors in the lives of women:

- Physiological: The monthly preparation of a woman's body for reproduction has no counterpart in men. Research and history confirm the debilitating effects of the premenstrual syndrome since earliest recorded times (puberty, pregnancy and menopause each deserve special attention.)

- Female Stress Symptoms: A particular set of conditions exclusively or most frequently affecting women has been well articulated by Dr. Georgia Wilkin-Lanoil. She identifies anorexia, bulimia, amenorrhea, frigidity, vaginismus, and unique anxiety reactions as well as special additions as constituting a female stress syndrome that begins in the womb ("Alcohol and HIV/AIDS").

- Socio-Cultural Conditioning: Fallacies about differences in the sexes begin in the earliest infancy. Adults perceive non-existent differences between boy and girl infants. A male baby wrapped in a pink blanket will be described by both sexes as more passive, crying, and less active than the same male baby when wrapped in the traditional baby blue blanket. These sexually attributed differences actually created separate realities for boys and girls. Women then carry an additional burden—the high price of sugar and spice.

These unique stressors are only a part of the picture of how women are affected on a daily basis. The women share a greater responsibility than men in most roles of life, including love, parenting, education, work, aging, and dying. Certainly HERstress could present a dismal picture. What then is the positive side? Surely women could not have survived these burdens over centuries without special supports.

How women use their exceptional strength, neurology, and coping skills to manage stress and general adaptation is a separate topic. Most importantly, the first step in stress education is to recognize the very real and dramatic array of stressors placed on women throughout their lives. Men and women both need a new consciousness for the daily and successful management of highly complex and challenging demands of HERstress.

When we add, like a Chinese menu, one from column A, etc., the last factor is the stress of new sobriety. Give yourself a break and begin today to learn healthy and sober ways of coping. Let's start with some ideas from women who've learned how to cope.

Would responsibility for $400 million dollars cause you stress? That's the amount that City of San Diego Treasurer, Conny oversees. How does this successful woman cope with on-the-job stress?

"I delegate. I try to always anticipate surprises by considering the areas of greatest risk and monitor those closely." Conny describes an effective system of communication both up and down the ladder of responsibility, so that she knows what is expected of her. She sends weekly reports to her boss, and receives them from her assistant department head. That way there are no imagined expectations.

Listening to advice from professionals has helped Conny, and knowing her job thoroughly reduces her daily stress. She also keeps it simple. "In the early years of my career, I chose a man's life style." She could not conceive of coping with children, husband, and family demands in the profession she had chosen. "I don't know how they (working mothers) do it." Recently married, she now has a chance to learn.

From the high-stress media industry, Lari Pomeroy, account executive, shares, "I've worked through my primary stress. It was fear, self-imposed fear. I had incredible expectations for myself, and fear of both failure and success." Lari learned to begin her day with 30 minutes of meditative and positive mental attitude readings. "Attitude adjustment is the key for me," she says. Lari also adjusted her eating habits. From erratic binging, the svelte executive gave up sugar and began three moderate meals a day with no weight gain. She had an immediate energy gain and began an exercise program. Most importantly, Lari began to reach out to other women. She began a women's 12-step support group in her home. "Caring about other women brought me to center. No longer concerned with self and fear, I increased my rapport with women. They and the experience of caring helped me to know that work is my excuse for the larger purpose of living, being, and caring."

Whether your job places you behind a desk, assembling electronic parts, selling products from your home, or in the boardroom, daily work stressors are a threat to mental and physical health. Here are some suggestions as we continue to focus on coping with nine-to-five stress:

- Break the cycle of stress: When you feel overwhelmed, stop. Coping with stress begins with a conscious effort to slow the momentum of demands, real or imagined, and pace work more realistically.
- Breathe: Under stress, breathing becomes more shallow and rapid, like panting. This is the beginning of hyperventilation. Chest pains can develop from overworking the diaphragm muscles. Breathe more deeply, consciously move your diaphragm. Count ten breaths.
- Change your position: If you are sitting, stand up and walk. When driving, consciously relax your grip on the steering wheel and sit back in the seat. Notice the bunched posture of

drivers under stress. If you are walking, slow down. If you can, sit for just a moment. Sit with both feet on the ground, arms at sides relaxed, and turn your palms up, resting hands in lap. Try it.

- Refocus: While driving, notice the sky, vistas, and pleasant surroundings. In a meeting, focus briefly on plants, artwork in the room, the view . . . remember, breaking the cycle takes only an instant.

- Reframe: When verbal demands are being made, try to restate the request. "Now as I understand you, you want . . ." Frequently, knowing what is clearly expected of us reduces stress. By reframing the task at hand, verbal interaction is slowed, messages are clear, and you gain time to plan a response.

- Practice, practice, practice: Now is the time to start. Ask yourself, "Am I breathing? Am I sitting in a relaxed posture as I read this?" Restate the messages in this book for yourself. Look around you at items which are visually pleasing. Now you're on the right track. To live is to experience stress. Stress on the job creates fatigue, mistakes, and is cumulative in its effect. Taking the first step, breaking the cycle of stress on the job will help you become a healthier and more personally productive woman.

10

YOUR JOB: ANTIDOTE TO STRESS

What about you and your job in sobriety? Working women face double-parody stress. The general life situations facing us all affect them. The dual burdens of work and home management affect them. Their physiology is cyclical and unique. Do all these demands add up to an impossible burden? Not at all.

The benefits of working outside the home are frequently the best and most often overlooked stress reducers available to women. To manage the dual stresses presented by dual roles, successful career women look to the positive in their jobs. They are then able to maintain sanity, and even a measure of serenity. What are the benefits of work that are the most significant in stress management? Let's take a look.

Support systems are very important in stress management. The work team, the department co-workers provide a built-in support group sharing both the burdens and the joys which place stress on women in their jobs and home.

Resources—those large pools of information readily available from co-workers—are great. Information ranging from career opportunities and Pre-Menstrual Syndrome to child-rearing and divorce attorneys is shared. The more knowledge we have, the more control we exercise—and the less we stress.

Social contracts are part of the day-to-day routine. Through the sharing of hard work, anxieties, defeats and victories, casual social interaction as well as lifelong friendships are facilitated. Meeting new people is a trite but very real advantage of working outside the home.

Confidants are readily available. Why is it often easier to tell an almost-stranger your personal problems than one who is close to you? Perhaps because they can be part of the solution rather than the problem. Workmates are people in whom you can confide. They, in turn, will confide in you, increasing your sense of self-worth and importance. Result: less stress.

Control is very important in stress reduction. A study of housewives and stress identified the lack of control over work demands as a major contributor to stress. Working women have greater degrees of control in their jobs, can set limits, and frequently control positive reinforcement. Again, more control, less stress.

Money is the primary gain from working. Whatever other benefits there may be, the salary earned by women is important in reducing stress. Women work for money, not for luxuries and fun. The salary earned is an important part of stress reduction.

Self-esteem is key to managing many roles successfully. Women who see themselves as capable are better able to manage dual roles than women who are equally capable but do not see themselves as such. The jobs which women perform can be a great source of pride, worth and self-esteem.

Actualization, whether in Maslow's hierarchy or your own, is a goal in work and management of our daily lives. Without creative outlets in the work environment, many women find it more difficult to maintain personal growth and self-actualization, so critical to their own happiness, and the happiness of those around them.

The benefits of working more than compensate for the additional stresses which jobs place on women. When things are tough, count your benefits. Turn to your workmates for help, advice and support. You will feel better, and you'll be better.

11

LIFE AS STRESS

To live is to experience stress. "The absence of stress," says noted researcher Hans Selye, "is death." It is obvious that death, illness, accidents and undesired changes will enter the lives of all women. The very positive events—marriage, having a baby, receiving a promotion, starting your own business, buying a home—also create stress. Do you actually know what causes stress in your life? There are hidden stresses which may surprise you. How much stress is too much?

To help you gain awareness of the stresses, and their impact on you, add up the points for each event or change that you have experienced in the past year. This Social Readjustment Scale of Life Events, developed by Thomas Holmes and Richard Rahe, may help you recognize hidden and new stresses. Your score can tell you how much HERstress is affecting you daily: A score of less than 150 indicates a slight risk of illness, up to 299 indicates moderate risk, and a score higher than 300 might mean you are at high risk for stress-related illness.

Social Readjustment Rating Scale

Life event	Life change units
Death of a spouse	100
Divorce	73
Marital separation	65
Imprisonment	63
Death of a close family member	63
Personal injury or illness	53
Marriage	50
Dismissal from work	47
Marital reconciliation	45
Retirement	45
Change in health of family member	44
Pregnancy	40
Sexual difficulties	39
Gain a new family member	39
Business readjustment	39
Change in financial state	38
Death of a close friend	37
Change to different line of work	36
Change in frequency of arguments	35
Major mortgage	32
Foreclosure of mortgage or loan	30
Change in responsibilities at work	29
Child leaving home	29
Trouble with in-laws	29
Outstanding personal achievement	28
Spouse starts or stops work	26

Life event	Life change units
Begin or end school	26
Change in living conditions	25
Revision of personal habits	24
Trouble with boss	23
Change in working hours or conditions	20
Change in residence	20
Change in schools	20
Change in recreation	19
Change in church activities	19
Change in social activities	18
Minor mortgage or loan	17
Change in sleeping habits	16
Change in number of family reunions	15
Change in eating habits	15
Vacation	13
Christmas	12
Minor violation of the law	11

(Holmes 2003)

12

COMBAT HOLIDAY STRESS

Holidays present a major stress challenge, especially in early recovery. Don't be surprised to find yourself already feeling a generalized anxiety in anticipation of the holidays that are months away. Guilt may be creeping into your thoughts. But don't feel alone. It is very normal to find the holidays stressful. Christmas is not always white and wonderful, but there is help. Let's examine HERstress and the holidays.

Begin at the source of stress. Schedules are disrupted—routines disturbed. Good and bad memories of past events return. Families begin to gather. Expectations start to build. Money is an immediate concern in many households. And, for the woman, studies show that it is she who carries the major responsibilities for decision making, entertaining, and the extra work of the holidays.

This season brings out the best and the worst in everyone. Frequently, adults and older children experience some regression to childhood behaviors. Eating too many goodies, wanting extra attention, expecting special presents and surprises, desiring perfection—we frequently dream of fantasy, not the real experience of Christmas. Our dreams are more often celluloid than reality—a picture in our minds.

- Awareness: This is the first step in coping. Knowing that you and your loved ones are under special stresses, emotions are charged, that extra work is part of the holidays, can help you be more patient and better prepared. Let's begin with planning.

- Holiday calendar: Take a large monthly calendar with boxes for each day for the next three months. Start with New Year's Day, Christmas, Hanukkah, or any other winter holiday, and move backwards. Mark the dates with what must be done that day—the tree trimmed, the dinner party, the cards mailed. Do not give yourself extra time as this will encourage procrastination. Mark the last possible date for the task to be completed. A task not completed by the date—is not done. Don't carry over.

- Lists: Lists can help us. Numbering to-do's, presents to buy, cards to send or goodies to be made can be helpful, but don't fool yourself. Lists can add stress by making tasks seem insurmountable. Also, we can add unnecessary items. We get carried away in our planning. Be conservative in your lists.

- Management systems: By now you are probably using a time management system. If you aren't, give yourself an early Christmas gift. It is important to manage activities as well as your time. Integrating all the holiday tasks and events into your system of daily management is an important step in being realistic about what you can accomplish.

- Focus on the positive: Remember what the holidays *do* bring. A break from work, a festive spirit, the sharing of gifts, food, and feelings. Each holiday has its own spiritual character. Save time to savor special moments. Participate in your own holiday.

- One moment at a time: Sound familiar? Yes, once again, remind yourself to take one moment at a time. Enjoy the extra work; take pleasure in the doing—not the outcome. Pause to enjoy the buying of a gift, the visual beauty of wrapping, the fun of sharing a holiday gift or remembrance. Know that some moments will be very special, others disappointing, and even painful. Take what you can from each.

- Memories: Holiday memories are good and bad. Try not to compare this season with previous holiday experiences. Each occasion stands alone. Make this one memorable for you, without expecting today to provide the same experience of past holidays.

- Let go: Holding on tightly to traditions may cause undue stress, extra work, and family tension. "We always have/do/take/go . . ." may stand in the way of relaxed enjoyment. Let go of traditions which may be too much work for your present resource. A fast-food picnic while trimming the tree may substitute for a full course family dinner that worked when the kids were younger and you weren't working. Children and teenagers frequently want to spend more time with their friends at this season. Tension may be created by forcing participation in traditional family activities that may no longer fit your lifestyle or theirs.

- Feast, laugh, and be comfortable: Have fun. Reduce stress by laughing. When all else fails, spend money. Call long-distance on Christmas Eve when you haven't mailed the greeting cards. Send a poinsettia to your mom on Christmas Day when you find the beautiful wrapped-for-mailing gift still in the trunk of your car. Light up your holiday, and everyone else's, with a smile.

How do women I interviewed combat holiday stress? Judy Stephens, freelance photographer, says, "No guilt. If it doesn't get done, you'll get a chance next year."

"Plan," says Johanna Strauss, a student at University of California at San Diego. "Most people say they want to be organized, but they don't. They like the 'rush' that chaos gives them."

And finally, from Dot Phillips, a homemaker, "Treat yourself gently. You deserve it."

Picture a greeting card. It's for Christmas, of course. A green frog smiles from a red background saying, "Happy Holidays." Inside, a cutout of another frog pops out, jiggling obscenely. The card reads, "From your offspring." This is the card I painstakingly selected for my father—totally neutral. No words of love, caring, acknowledgment of what he's done for my life, how he's contributed to my success, how much I miss him. No emotion.

You'd think by now Hallmark would have gotten the message. Why haven't the greeting card companies come up with a section of cards for children from dysfunctional families? Just think, no more searching for a card which doesn't use the word "love" on Mother's Day: ideally, cards which make no mention of how much you care for your parents. Cards which are so bland as to be marked down in price and slightly dog-eared from being passed over by Adult Children of Normal Environments.

Can't you see it? Sections for every holiday possibility—"Greetings to my overeating mother on her day. No chocolate for you, sweetie, but keep coming back."

Or to my alcoholic dad on Father's Day: "Hi Pop. I'm not following in your footsteps. Ready to go to a meeting yet?" Family history, memories, concerns and issues often preoccupy the mind of a recovering person during the holiday season. No other calendar event seems quite such a slippery place. This month I want to address "Family Forgiveness and the Holidays."

What makes this topic especially deviant to women? Women have most of the holiday caretaking responsibilities. If you're a single mom, you may have had it all in the past few months. That means addressing the cards, cooking, shopping for presents, wrapping, and mailing. It means post office lines, list-making, organizing, and peace-keeping as tension mounts. Holidays also mean a burden of memories, expectations, disappointments, and fears. The high emotions feed into the estrogen-based, emotionally changeable physiology of women.

Recently, my friend Dick W. shared his Christmas card fantasy of the holidays. He pictured rosy-cheeked children gathered around a fireplace. Their sober, loving parents look on as gifts were opened in a snow-covered cottage which glowed with warmth and love. That had never happened for him. And yet, each December, that picture comes to his mind. For most of us, the reality does not match the picture. Our family gatherings were often characterized by ugly scenes, angry dialogues, sometimes violence, disappointments, and despair.

From the sound of the first note of "Silent Night," expectations start to build. "Will it be different this year?" "Will it be perfect?" "Can't everyone pitch in and be a family, just for once?"

Holidays seem to bring out the best and the worst in everyone. At the same time we're planning gifts and caring activities, adults begin to act like children, and children act worse. We regress to childish behaviors. We eat too much—especially sugar—want extra attention, expect perfect presents as well as surprises, whine and complain, resent the extra work, make unrealistic demands on ourselves, overspend, and punch credit to the limit.

Just like Scrooge in Dickens' *A Christmas Carol*, I personally am drawn into Christmas past. I am forced (or think I am) to deal with my abusive, alcoholic father, and other family members that have contributed significantly to my own problems with living sober.

As I stood picking out the frog card, I found myself once more examining my feelings about the father who had violently battered my two brothers and me. Like sticking my tongue into the cavity of a decayed tooth, I checked to see if the pain is still there. Is it still as sharp? Worse? Or has it, by some miracle, gone away? Yes, the pain is still there.

So what can I do to cope with future holiday seasons and all these feelings?

Let's start by letting ourselves off the hook. Look forward to the brightness of Christmas Future. Create for yourself new memories, the beginning of a new family history. Here are some ideas for coping with memories and the "Ghost of Christmas Past":

- Try "self-talk": When your head starts playing the memories, expectations and resentments from the past, begin talking out loud—just describe what's around you: the ice plant on the freeway, the kitchen cabinets . . . talk out loud until your mind stops projecting. Like a camera, you can refocus.
- Say the gratitude alphabet: A, I'm grateful for (AA, apples, alimony). B, I'm grateful for (*Big Book*, boys, bubble bath). C, I'm grateful for (chocolate, my computer) . . . and so on.
- Put your watch on the other wrist for a day: Remember a thought or behavior change you want to make each time you look at the wrong wrist.

- Let go of projecting: Think of a movie projector throwing an image to a screen. It isn't real and yet hundreds of people sit and watch it. What your mind projects is not real. Stay in the moment.

- What about a holiday gift for God or your Higher Power? Could that be the gift of family forgiveness? Perhaps the gift of your anger, your shame, and the pain those memories evoke in you. If your tree is still up, try actually wrapping a gift for your Higher Power and putting it underneath it. It could contain a letter about your feelings, a picture of your worst memory. Maybe it should be empty, symbolizing the letting go of bad memories, of the family past. Make this a gift for yourself, the gift of self-forgiveness.

- Last but not least, I'd like to give all of you two gifts—my thanks for all the wonderful letters, comments, and suggestions for this book over the past year—and my wishes for you for the peace, happiness, and joy of sober living in the new year to come, during the holidays, or at any other time.

"Life can only be understood backwards. But it must be lived forwards." If Soren Kierkegaard hadn't said this first, I'm sure Bill W. would have.

13

How Your Body Reacts

The physical effects of stress appear as dramatic warnings. High blood pressure, heart attack, chronic fatigue, and loss of appetite head the list. Or it can manifest quite the opposite. Low blood pressure, compulsive overeating, and excess energy can be the picture; research shows us that we are vulnerable to illness under stress. Cold, flu, depression, accidents, and ill-defined aches and pains seem to affect us when we are least prepared physically to fight them off. Stress ages us, make us impotent, fearful, irritable—even dangerous.

Identifying stressors in our lives usually focuses on agents outside the body: fear, pressure, anxiety—which affect our minds. The mind triggers certain physiological reactions in the body in response to these agents of stress. While the stressors may be abstract or difficult to define, they are clear in the body's reaction. Many of the effects of stress are chemical in nature. When danger messages travel from the brain to the body, they travel in three channels:

1. Motor messages: In preparation to fight or run, the brain alerts arms, legs, and muscles, creating tension and movement.

2. Metabolism messages: The autonomic nervous system takes over, elevating blood pressure, heart beat and blood sugar (slowing digestion).

3. Stimulant messages: Adrenaline is released as a general stimulant. Glands other than the adrenal are activated producing hormonal changes, affecting salt and water balance, and increasing the white blood cell count.

On a daily basis (no matter how rushed you are) prepare those three channels through which the ALERT message will travel:

- Stretch the motor channel: Take a few moments each morning to loosen arms and legs. The danger messages exert the same pressure as vigorous exercise without warm-up. Yoga, breathing, or just simple stretching will all help.

- Shake out the stress during the day: Like a rag doll, shake your arms and legs loosely and gently. Lift shoulders and relax. Keep breathing.

- Snack out the metabolism: Yes, the dreaded snack-attack. Keep adrenaline and blood sugar in balance by eating little and often. Saltines, raisins and cereals will keep the rush of stress at bay. If you have regular meal habits, leave lots of time for digestion before entering the "arena."

- Avoid stimulant overdose: Your body will be producing shots of stimulation during the day. Don't overdose on caffeine, sugar, or other stimulants including diet drinks. Increase water intake.

How do people I interviewed experience the physical aspects of stress? Jan W. who prepares tax returns says, "It hits me in the stomach. I try to go with the feeling. I drink club soda, but mostly I have learned that acceptance is the key. I don't try to control the situation and that is really working."

Nancy Mullins, artist and young mother, reports, "My shoulders begin to pull up toward my ears. I don't realize what is happening and suddenly I look like a no-neck. I pull my shoulders down with my hands while breathing deeply."

14

WHAT IS THE I.S.?

The Immune System (I.S.) recognizes *us* from *them*. It identifies self from foreign bodies which enter our bodies. Luckily it functions like a well-trained Doberman (and not like my cocker spaniel Gatsby) when intruders appear on the scene. It destroys invaders and then clears the wreckage of the present to keep the body healthy. Key players in this drama (which fortunately operate automatically without our control) include: Natural killer cells, T and B Helper cells, and Pac-Man-like Gobbler cells. It's an exciting scene—appealing to the alcoholic's flair for drama.

B and T Helper cells lie in the body's filter system waiting for foreign substances to destroy. The Gobblers surround invaders like aliens, with tentacles and amoeba-like movements, digesting viruses, and sending the residue out like a character defect following a searching and fearless 5th Step.

Some of this drama produces observable symptoms of illness. We cough and sneeze, run fevers, crave teddy bears, and eat chicken soup. We whine and complain. Hurrah. The system is working.

There are many familiar conditions, such as Chronic Fatigue Syndrome, the common cold, herpes, and mononucleosis, that may be brought on by depression of the I.S. Activities of daily living can weaken and damage the I.S. A factor we'll call EBV measures resistance to these conditions. EBV levels go up or down depending on what we do and how we think. Some of these activities and situations especially affect women. In the next chapter, let's take a look at some current research findings and directions to help you understand how stress affects your ability to ward off illness and disease, conditions which not only affect our bodies, but our minds.

15

RESEARCH LOOKS AT LIFE

Let's begin with the dreaded R-word. Relationships. The ending of relationships has several specific and adverse effects on a woman's I.S. Divorce or ending a relationship produces many immediate and negative effects in the face of longer-term positive outcomes. I.S. effects include:

- A lowering of the number of Natural killer cells
- Poorer immune control
- Decrease in the production of Interferon (a fighter of viruses)

The greater the attachment to the partner, the poorer the resultant function. In other words, the more you love someone, the greater the health risk in divorce or ending the attachment. Additionally, for relationships and marriages which don't end in separation or divorce, but are of poor quality, the effects on women are still severe, including:

- Depression
- Chronic fatigue
- Higher incidence of EBV (a condition associated with the common cold and mononucleosis)
- Decrease in the proliferation of the "good" white cells (Natural killers, T and B Helpers)

This has many important implications for the alcoholic or co-dependent who seems to have little understanding of the word "over." The obvious action step is a resolution of problems or ending a relationship quickly when it no longer meets healthy standards.

Men don't exactly thrive in similar situations, but those who initiate the ending have a lower EBV count, or less susceptibility to fatigue, common cold, and mono. For non-initiators, the EBV rate goes up. Men in situations of marital distress have measurably lower "T," or helper cells.

So what, you say. Separation, ending a distressful relationship and divorce can't be avoided. The "so what" danger is two-fold:

1. Resolve relationship problems to reduce health consequences.
2. Pay special attention to your I.S. during periods of relationship stress and transition.

If you and your partner can't resolve conflicts, re-establish communication and sexual intimacy, then you may need professional help. Certainly your program sponsor and close friends may have suggestions. Marriage counselors, therapists, ministers, spiritual advisors, and couples groups are all resources. Get into action before your T and B Helpers, Gobblers and Natural killers are in greater deficit.

Here are some other stressful situations that have specific Immune System effects:

Studies of medical students the day before an exam show these students have measurably decreased levels of Helper cells, Interferon, and Natural killers. Their EBV levels increase (remember, this condition makes you more susceptible to colds). Other studies produce similar results in the face of common stresses. Family members caring for an Alzhiemer's patient have reduced Helper T-cells. Soldiers facing simulated battle have a dual response—an increase of Interferon (a good effect) but reduced Gobbler cells (a bad effect). Those of us facing stormy situations like a simulated battle should take heed.

And how about your state of mind? Depression, a condition affecting women five times more than men, results in higher EBV, lower proliferation of the "good" cells, and faster HIV progression (for those affected). Loneliness lowers the count of Natural killers, increased EBV and lowers Helper count. Along this same line, people judged as more extroverted have fewer colds (EBV factor).

Finally, poor coping skills, such as sleeping or shopping in response to stress, reduces Helper T-cells, increases Herpes outbreaks for those affected, and interferes with progress on life goals. An ongoing poor coping ability, continuous subjecting of the I.S. to the fight/flight syndrome, suppresses the production of good CD4 cells. Again, our overall approach to daily living and commitment to a healthy lifestyle directly affects the body's ability to ward off disease.

So, while it is perhaps old news that stress affects our minds and bodies negatively, these studies show direct relationships between our life choices and damage to the I.S. The good news is that by reversing or shortening traumatic events and increasing coping skills, the reverse effects are often achieved, or at least the system is not being damaged.

Here are the results of some intervention studies. In experiments with relaxation training, relaxed subjects produced higher levels of Helper T cells and Natural killers. When the relaxation techniques were stopped, the levels returned to baseline.

Do you hate it when friends, therapists, or sponsors ask, "Did you write about it?" Ugh. Well, writing about traumatic events (and for us alcoholics, that may be chipping a $2 acrylic fingernail) for 20 minutes increased Helper T cell production, and decreased the number of visits for health care. This research fits in perfectly with the wisdom of AA. The written 4th Step, or a 20 minute evening ritual writing a 10th Step, can actually strengthen your I.S. (not to mention your recovery.)

As I listened to this impressive array of how-tos, I was secretly amused. The lovely, erudite woman research was outlining our 12-step programs. See what you think.

- Eat healthy: Good nutrition continues to be directly related to I.S. function. Reduce fat and increase fiber.

- Reduce caffeine and have sex: Contrary to popular opinion you can stay sober without coffee (I'm not sure about the sex) and your I.S. will be better off. Same with smoking, overeating and other bad habits, ad nauseam. Luckily, sex is good for you. Yes, orgasm produces a unique endorphin that enhances the coping response to stress. Great idea and fun for all.

- Provide support to others: This suggestion directly relates to another 12-step necessity, including service work in your program of stress management, not only within the 12-step program. What about community service? There are many H&I or public service committee activities, volunteering at non-profit recovery programs, or finding community involvement where you can serve as an alcohol and drug-free role model. Try Big Brothers and Big Sisters, or the United Way.

- Increase the quality of intimate relationships: Consider working it out with your existing partner—so what if he's not "perfect?" Does he have the capacity to make you feel good? How can you re-kindle those feelings? So what if she's obsessed with her new job? What good feelings did you have when you first fell in love (or lust)? Go back to when the relationship was working and re-enact those early courtship activities.

- Train for tragedy: Are you anticipating a traumatic event? I certainly hope not. No—this refers to studying for exams as an example, getting married (positive stress), anticipating bereavement (death of a friend or family member). If you are, get into training. Studies show that of several techniques including social contacts (sharing with friends, being in groups), the most effective was formal relaxation training carried out by the individual at home. This significantly increased I.S. changes for the better. Some of these effects, including increasing Natural killer cells, lasted as long as six months.

- Coping with challenges: Discuss feelings and traumatic events immediately and more than once. At a 12-step meeting, share the trauma but not the drama. Skip the gory (and boring) details, but share the feelings. Write about the problem. Sharpen a pencil and boost that production. Besides improving your resistance to disease, better coping can improve your sober lifestyle.

- Reduce passive strategies: Are you perpetually late? Stop passively punishing those around you. Are you underachieving on the job? Still showing your pushy mother, huh? Watching TV while you're on the phone listening to a boring drama/

trauma from a friend? Tell her the truth. Don't go to sleep when unhappy, get active. Recognize your passively aggressive strategies and change your behavior. Your sponsor can help with steps 6 and 7. Studies showed that animals who exhibit submissive behaviors in response to domination have weaker Immune Systems. In one species of fish, the submissive ones are forced to live upside-down. If that reminds you of a work or personal situation—change it. Get your life and I.S. sunny-side up.

- Increase control over controllable events: I smiled as I listened to this famous medical research describing our old stand-by, "The Serenity Prayer." A cure? Not quite, but another brick in the foundation of a healthy Immune System—and your personal recovery program.

- Handle aspects of your life which lead to defeat: Does overeating lead to depression? Of course. Does irrational and unresolved anger lead to depression? Absolutely. Does cleaning the bathroom depress me—sure does. I wait until I have to wear tennis shoes in the shower before I clean the tub. Stop defeating yourself by engaging in activities which depress you. Sometimes professional help may be needed. Try visiting a therapist or counselor to get an overview of what may be needed to change a specific behavior. Talk to trusted friends and sponsors. Keep a journal specifically aimed at connecting your actions and subsequent feelings to self-defeat.

- Maintain (or build) self-esteem: For my faithful readers you know this means . . . . yes, cleaning out the underwear drawer. Build your foundation on silk. Dump your cotton favorites, giant safety pin and all. That color's not French Gray—it's designer dinge. Work on your feelings of worth and value. One of our loyal male readers, Jeff W. (recovering alcoholic and jazz aficionado) says the equivalent for him is car maintenance. He feels better about himself when his upholstery is Armor-allied and the engine cleaned and shined.

- Assess priorities and focus on life goals: Isn't it time to face career issues? Do you want/need to improve your education? Go after that degree. Take a risk on setting up the food truck you always wanted. Start an online t-shirt business or do marketing consulting if that is your ambition. Find role models whose lives and careers attract you. Ask them how they did it. Stick with the winners.

Or maybe it's time to make personal commitments. Do you really want to be married and have kids? Is it time to end a dead-end and unfulfilling relationship? Identify satisfying and fulfilling life goals for happiness and a stronger I.S.

16

A New Beginning

How can I summarize a 10-hour day filled with complex medical terms, detailed scientific data, rapidly changing statistics, and the trauma of epidemic conditions affecting national health? The preventative measures still relate to a phrase we hear often in AA meetings: "This is a selfish program." To live life with health and freedom from chronic illness as well as deadly disease, put you first. Find the balance between work, play, social, and spiritual activities. Give up bad habits and compulsive behaviors. Commit to life goals which constitute your dreams. Begin today, and one day at a time live a life with purpose, integrity and joy. Perhaps Walter B.'s favorite maxim sums up the conference findings: "For today well-lived makes every yesterday a dream of happiness, and every tomorrow a vision of hope. Look then to this day, for it is life."

A cartoon I recently saw showed an attractive young woman, stereotypically buxom, marooned on a desert island. The caption read, "Safe Sex." The interpretations certainly boggle the mind—are women only safe from men when stranded? Are women the safe sex?

Are men only safe when women are isolated? Whether the cartoon is funny or not, it touched the confusion I personally feel on the topic of "Women and AIDS." This very serious disease has particular and tragic implications for women, and particularly for recovering women.

The problem of AIDS is that the population of heterosexual women has a lot in common with alcoholism in women—it's hard for society to accept that wives, mothers, sisters, and daughters end up in drunken tanks and worse. It seems equally difficult to accept the prospect of AIDS in that same population.

Between 55, 000 and 60, 000 people in the United States become infected with HIV every year ("HIV among Women"). According to the Centers for Disease Control and Prevention, women make up that 24 percent of all diagnoses and 20 percent of AIDS diagnoses in the United States. The most common transmission methods were heterosexual contact and injection drug use (Reece 2010).

The relationship between AIDS and IV drug use seems well-accepted by the media and general public. But the well-documented link to alcoholism is less publicized. Clearly a person who is in denial about her own drinking is at high risk for:

- Secrecy and isolation in personal life
- Lowered inhibitions in sexual situations
- Poor judgment in partner selection and experience
- Multiple partners and one-night stands
- Sexual abuse including rape
- Poor health care and attention
- Inability to control outcomes and consequences

But the recovering woman also experiences special risk factors beyond those of other women. The most influential of those is denial.

For most of us who are recovering, the defense mechanism of denial does not stop working just because we've stopped drinking and using. For Adult Children of Alcoholics and co-dependent women, and the so-called "triple and quadruple winners"—the risk factors associated with denial also multiply.

Condom use is a known preventative method in contacting HIV/AIDS and other sexually transmitted diseases, yet a majority of the population does not practice safe sex. The National Survey of Sexual Health and Behavior conducted one of the most comprehensive studies in almost two decades concerning condom-use behaviors. The study included 5, 865 adolescents and adults ages 14-94 and what they found was only one in four sexual acts are actually protected in the United States. Interestingly, the data concluded that many contemporary adolescents were either abstaining from sex or using condoms and adults over the age of 40 had the lowest rates of condom use (Reece 2010).

In another study, a sizable group of men said they might be unwilling to tell their partners about testing HIV positive. 12 percent said they would not tell their primary partners and 29 percent would not tell their non-primary partners. Women face double jeopardy in these two examples: their own denial systems coupled with deception on the part of their partners.

Further, let's look at how women experience sexual abuse. Today's statistics indicate one in four women has experienced sexual abuse by age 18. Between 60 to 80 percent of codependent women have experienced incest. Isn't it likely that sexual coercion short of abuse, date rape, and other abuse may be much, much higher? Relationship dependency, sexual addiction, and simply "terminal" non-assertiveness greatly multiply the risk of women having unprotected high-risk sex.

17

NEXT STEP

I too am affected by the denial, "It-can't-happen-to-me" syndrome. But today I'm not willing to take the risk. As a sober woman, I have too much to live for.

So let me tell you quite frankly I have been to Costco all by myself and purchased condoms treated with Non-oxynol-9. Yes, it was embarrassing and took a lot of nerve, but they're everywhere: in grocery stores, on the mail order pages of Cosmo, even in the health food store near the granola bars. But I did it and I'm okay. I have since found condoms on a key chain, condoms in fortune cookies, generic condoms, "Pet Rubbers," and designer earrings which double as condom concealers.

Here are some ideas to help you take control of sexual consequences:

- Education, not morality: Inform yourself through education, reading pamphlets, books, and magazines. Many can be ordered through the mail and from toll-free numbers. Don't be caught up in other people's denial or their opinions and possible misinformation.

- Purchase condoms: Grab a friend and go for it. Either through mail order, male friends, or your own courage, make condoms a part of your sex life.

- Monogamous partner testing: If you and your partner are committing to monogamous sex, consider testing. As you begin a new monogamous relationship, indicate your willingness to undergo AIDS testing and ask your partner to do the same, especially men in high-risk categories—alcoholics and addicts, of course.

- Keep it light: Practice your dialogue with a woman friend. Many booklets suggest phrases. Remember, this is not a personal issue just a statistical one. Keep your sense of humor but be firm—before you get to the bedroom ("Your condom or mine?").

Share H.O.W.—Honestly, Openly and Willingly share concern, education, and prevention with others—your adolescent children, friends, and sponsees. The public library has excellent books and pamphlets to help children of all ages. If you have sexually active kids, help them keep prevention a part of their lives.

Finally, becoming comfortable with the reality, the facts of STDs—incidence, transmission, and risks—are an essential component of prevention. Becoming comfortable with new attitudes, changing practices, and facing your fears may take time. But your investment, one-step at a time, will insure not only personal health and safety, but the containment of this unfortunate disease.

18

ACHIEVING SERENITY

African chicken feathers . . . soaking in steaming hot sulfur springs . . . barbecued tofu . . . meeting around a late night camp fire . . . myriad stars and burned s'mores . . . . sand painting . . . medicine bundles . . . solitude . . . . nature walks . . . . waterfall sounds . . . . sunset darkening the valley below. What kind of recipe is this, you ask? One for serenity, I answer.

I remember when I had the pleasure of co-facilitating a retreat. There were activities designed to help us let go of the destructive patterns of the past and manage stress. We used Navajo and Hopi practices to focus group interaction. Participants used primitive art techniques to create medicine bundles with their own special spirit guides, listened to haunting music from animal bone flutes, painted with sands brought from the desert and used solitude in a very special way.

As a facilitator, I went there to work. As a recovering woman, I succumbed to the magic of the mountains. I relaxed and stayed to play.

Notice I don't mention jangling phones, traffic jams, gridlock, Pepto-Bismol, or daily hysteria. There was very little stress. Our meals were beautiful, and served (by someone else) on time. There was no jostling in the grocery store, banging carts with stubborn wheels, or trying to rent a car without 29 forms of ID. Beds were comfortable (made by someone else) with clean, cotton sheets and fluffy towels abounded. The swimming pool was inviting around the clock (no clogged filters or weekend scrubbing). There was lots of free time (no one whined, "Mooother . . . ."), no bills were overdue, and no one asked me to work overtime. The sunsets were perfect (no driving, no smog, no crowded beach).

Who wouldn't be able to control stress in this environment? The most commonly asked question from participants was, "How do I take this home? What am I supposed to do when my boss starts shouting? Tickle him with my chicken feather? Pull out my medicine bundle and meditate? How does this work in the real world?"

Most of us have more than one full-time job. The stress of dual roles, work and mothering, working and caretaking, is well-publicized if not well-understood. Many of us haven't handled that problem when we come to recovery. In fact, caretaking may be what was keeping us level, over-working was protecting our jobs, and superwoman activities were keeping the family at least tolerant; constant work took us away from the fear of what was happening to our lives.

In sobriety we add another full-time job—recovering. Particularly in early recovery, that term means exactly what it says—full-time. But, you say, that's unrealistic, my family and job have to take a lot of my time. If I don't keep them, I'll have lost everything. How can I make extra time? Who can go off and climb mountains and watch sunsets? I can't sand-paint in the staff meeting.

The word which came to my mind as I listened to the participants say what wouldn't work for them was priority. Too often we use other people and work as an excuse for doing what is best for us. What will happen if you sit in a bubble bath for 15 minutes? Oh, wow, you say. The kids will smear peanut butter on the windows and break the furniture. Yes, maybe they will. And those same children may have to help clean and use allowances to pay for new lamps. You may have to re-train those around you. In order to stop caretaking, you may have to teach others, spouses and family members, friends and co-workers, how to take care of themselves.

This weekend reminded me that only I can set priorities if I intend to take control of my time. Too often I let the telephone, co-workers, family members, even strangers, dictate my priorities, feelings—my state of mind. Just for today, I'm going to change that.

Just for today, I'm going to stick my African chicken feather in my purse and touch its gentleness during the day. Just for today, I'm going to make breakfast from that oatmeal and apple recipe Rosemary gave me. Just for today, I'm going to lay my medicine bundle on the top of my desk to remind me of the peace I felt this weekend. Just for today, I'm going to put myself first and be proud of how far I've come. Just for today, I'm going to choose to feel great—and remember it really is just one day at a time. Just for today, I know that yesterday is but a dream, and tomorrow is only a vision. But today, well lived, makes every yesterday a vision of hope. Look well to this day.

19

ALONE. BUT NOT LONELY

Recently I sat in a discussion meeting listening to the touching story of a young woman who had recently "slipped"—she drank again after a year of happy and joyous sobriety. She talked about how she stopped going to meetings and said, "I began to isolate." We hear that phrase often in the shared experience of recovering people: "I didn't want to call anyone, I just wanted to isolate."

Toward the end of my own drinking and using, I lived in isolation. The pain of loneliness and feeling alone was so severe I could feel it like the worst toothache or stomach cramp. I would stare out my bedroom window (when I didn't have the curtains drawn) looking at people going about the business of living and wonder how they did it. I would make long-distance calls to former friends and tell them ad nauseam how sad my life was, and how none of it was my fault.

The word "isolation" comes from the French word meaning "island." And that is what I wanted—to be alone on an island. In my mind-altered state, I withdrew from all meaningful social contact. I avoided any sort of intimacy because it risked revealing the extent of my drinking and using.

Now in recovery, all that is behind me. But like many recovering people, the feeling and fears come back from time to time.

Of all natural human emotions, loneliness can be one of the most painful and paralyzing. For recovering people, loneliness is a real threat to sobriety. It is so important it is even part of the familiar H.A.L.T. rule that has helped many in recovery get through a difficult day: "Never get too Hungry, Angry, Lonely, or Tired." I can't emphasize it enough.

We all experience loneliness during our lives. We could call it the negative side of our human need for closeness and contact with others, and beliefs that make us feel comfortable and whole.

The feeling of loneliness is like an alarm in our human warning system. It tells us that somehow our lives are out of balance and something needs attention. We need to take some action to restore the sense of peace that is natural and necessary to a fulfilling life. For lonely people, truly admitting those feelings is the first step.

In the beginning, admitting our loneliness can make the problem seem endless and unsolvable. Often we will cover our lonely feelings with depression or anger. But depression just limits our ability or desire to take action to change our lives, and anger makes us act inappropriately as we attempt to ease our loneliness. This just makes the situation worse.

Many people throw themselves into frantic activity or an exciting relationship as a cover-up or distraction. There may even be thoughts of returning to using drugs or overeating to end the pain of isolation. If we have done this in the past, we may be tempted to continue the quick fix pattern. It may be hard to remember these fixes are temporary. We will have to begin all over again when the fix wears off and loneliness overwhelms us again.

No one can expect to live a life completely free of occasional feelings of loneliness. But what now seems like an endless future of emptiness and isolation can become a productive period of growth and change. For that to happen we will need to understand our feelings and to consider appropriate actions that will help us feel better. The keys are understanding and appropriate action.

Think for a moment about your earliest experiences of loneliness when you were young and remember how you felt. It may be very much the way you are feeling now. Many of our early experiences as children affect how we deal with loneliness as adults.

Probably very few people had an ideal, completely happy childhood. We who have experienced the pain of addiction are not likely to have had good care while growing up. We had the same human needs to be loved, held, and reassured. But for reasons beyond our control, our needs were met poorly or not met at all. We never learned that loneliness is a temporary situation, not an endless, painful one.

An alcoholic parent may have made the family setting very uncertain. We were loved one minute and abandoned the next. Both parents may have had to work long hours and had little time or energy for their children, or emotional problems may have prevented a parent from showing affection.

If we don't have a secure beginning in childhood, we are much more likely to suffer panic and pain from loneliness when we are adults. The fear of abandonment was never resolved for us, and we continue to suffer as adults.

Children from dysfunctional families can suffer from self-imposed isolation. They withdraw from dangerous or hurtful situations. Fearful or shy children may hide in a safe place in the house, or they may hide in schoolwork or other solitary activities. When we carry these habits through into our adult lives, we live a numbed existence. We never challenge the belief that to reach out means to be hurt. The fear of reaching out becomes greater than the hope for a reward.

Sometimes children in dysfunctional families have to grow up too fast. They start taking care of other family members if the adults cannot. This more subtle isolation can also make a child feel different and lonely—cut off from a normal childhood.

But the most common feeling—in fact, part of the definition of loneliness—is a sense of loss or craving. It is a sad desire for something or someone we long for.

Children from dysfunctional families can be victims of an endless number of situations that interfere with a natural sense of security and peace. If the problems are never solved during childhood, the feelings are carried inside and the isolated child becomes the lonely adult.

Okay, you say, we all feel isolation and know that it can be a slippery place. What should I do when I begin to withdraw, to feel that I've heard it all in meetings—that I just want to be alone?

These feelings are an early warning that something in our lives needs to be changed, that action is the next step. The importance of a solid foundation in recovery can't be overemphasized in this regard. If we've laid a firm foundation, service work is part of that. Reaching out to others, establishing yourself as a source of help and comfort is the beginning of feeling better, more whole, and part of the human race.

While we can put the booze and drugs away, the feelings that came to us as children, long before we began to drink, are not easy to handle. Listen to your early warning system. Don't ignore a feeling of loneliness hoping it will go away. Take action through service and help to others. Get to a meeting and share your feelings.

And be grateful. These feelings, no matter how painful, are part of living. Today, we are alive—not anesthetized, not sedated, not passed out. Take control of your feelings and through action you can change. Today, as every day of sober living, we have a choice.

20

SURRENDER TO WIN:
YOU'VE GIVEN EVERYTHING BUT UP

It is said that the three most essential qualities in anyone's recovery are honesty, open-mindedness, and willingness. Without these we cannot hope to gain the freedom offered in the 12 Steps of recovery. When we made the decision to seek help in any one of many anonymous programs, we had already admitted we could no longer go on as we had, that we needed help from somewhere. This is part of the 1st Step of recovery, admitting powerlessness over our addictions and recognizing that we can no longer manage our own lives. We found this relatively easy to do, since the evidence was overwhelming for most of us.

Resistance, or ego, returned when we were asked to recognize a power greater than ourselves and then to turn our will and our lives over to that Higher Power. Surely this was insanity; "If I can't manage my life, how can something I can't even see or that I don't believe in do a better job?" Successfully recovering people have found through experience that this act of exchange, or letting go, was essential.

The first and most valuable tool we have as recovering people is the 12-step program. Each step forms a base of support that leads us to a more thorough self-discovery and, eventually, a spiritual awakening. Then we can reach out and help others like ourselves to find freedom. The 1ˢᵗ Step teaches us that we must surrender absolutely and completely our addictions in order to live. How many times have you heard someone in a meeting say, "I never want to forget where I came from. I have to remind myself almost daily what life was like before I came here. Otherwise I get complacent and for me, complacency equals death." This act of surrender then forms the basis for which we approach each of the consecutive steps, never forgetting just what it felt like to let go and give up the suicidal path we had been traveling.

In working each of the steps, or looking at them as a whole if you are a beginner, take a piece of paper and make a list of what it is you feel you should, or have been, told to surrender. Remember that this is a form of exchange. On the same paper, write the things that you think might be desirable in exchange for what you are surrendering. Here is an example:

Surrender:	Exchange for:
Drinking and using	Fellowship of meetings
Hangovers	Feeling healthy
Atheism	Openness to belief
False power	Manageability

There's a machine which has been proven to be 100 percent effective in the fight against addiction—the telephone. Call your sponsor, a friend, or just pick a number off that list you have from your Tuesday meeting. Marisa M. remembers her feelings before opening up about her addiction: "I just couldn't. I'd be bothering them and besides, I doubt if they'd even want to talk to me. They don't want to hear my problems." Sometimes the hardest things to surrender are insecurity and pride. We still think it's weak to ask for someone else's help. We're still out here waging the "me against the world" war. Be honest, once again. How many battles have you won with your "me, myself, and I" army? Take a deep breath and call.

Have you ever had one of those days when you've got nothing to wear, you're thinking of selling your kids through the classifieds, your only criterion for a man in your life is that he doesn't eat with his fingers, and you feel about as secure as a drugstore hair extension? Well, I have. Many of the issues facing recovering women have to do with controlling and juggling responsibilities and obligations. In this juggling act, it is easy to lose sight of the "me" and that primary goal—sobriety. Giving up control while still accomplishing the tasks of daily living may seem an impossible paradox. In *Surrender to Win*, I have tried to give specific exercises to help women see how surrender can help make their lives manageable.

"When I first went to a meeting, they told me that sobriety came first. They said that going to meetings was more important than working. Since I know my livelihood, and my family depended on working, I put that first. I thought these people didn't understand." In this example, perhaps the speaker might have listed "my job, concerns of family financial security, and the future of employment" as things she must surrender in order to face her alcoholism. Surrender in this case related to fears and activities which might have interfered with putting a program of sobriety first.

Do the exercise for each of the steps. The idea is just to begin to think in terms of not only giving, but receiving. Receiving is very hard for alcoholics and addicts. They are great givers, but often fear that if they want or ask for the good, they will somehow become vulnerable. Go ahead, try this.

21

MY EXPERIENCE

In my own life as a therapist, owner of my own business, single parent, and single woman, I know how difficult it is to balance and set priorities. Often, before sobriety, I used drugs to help me achieve those superhuman efforts that were needed to juggle so many demands. It has been very hard in sobriety for me to learn to say no, to put myself first, and to keep a clear focus on sober living.

Women face unique problems with surrender. Their place in this male dominated society, power structure, and recovery program has too often required them to submit in order to survive. Problems with self-esteem, ego strength, and assertiveness confuse the process of learning to surrender: "Haven't I already done that too much?"

Perhaps on those days when you feel too powerless to take a next step you'll try this exchange exercise. Give up some control for a measure of serenity. Make your lists and share your feelings with a friend. As Bill said, "Only through utter defeat are we able to take our first steps toward liberation and strength. Our admissions of personal powerlessness finally turn out to be the firm bedrock upon which happy, purposeful lives may be built."

This is a lot like faking it, but requires a little more effort and insight. Sometimes we may identify something we need to surrender, but just can't seem to make the break. It's too important or perhaps it's something we think only we can take care of, like your relationship with your husband or wife. Maybe it's your job. Maybe it's the creditors that are harassing you. Well, you can continue to carry these milestones about your neck or you can act "as if." Act "as if" you no longer had a need to be right when you argue with your spouse. Act "as if" you are not angry and resentful when your boss schedules you to work on Saturday night. Act "as if" you no longer feel guilty when you get an overdue notice from a collection agency. In other words, act "as if." This is a useful way into the back door to surrender.

Indulge your inflated ego once in a while, but in a different way. Instead of fantasizing about grandiose schemes and perfectionist plans, actually treat yourself like a king or queen for a while. Take a few hours to enjoy a bubble bath, a movie, or book. Veg out, chill out, cut yourself some slack—in general, give yourself a break. It is okay to try to escape an uncomfortable situation. Change is often uncomfortable. A break can help you accept sober responsibilities with renewed energy.

If you find yourself getting into frequent quarrels with people, feeling obstinate and defiant, remember, that's the way frustrated children behave. Stand your ground on what you know is right, but do so calmly and make allowance for the fact that you could turn out to be wrong and even if you're dead right, it's easier on your system to give in once in a while. If you yield, others will too. The result will be relief from tension, the achievement of a practical solution, together with a great feeling of satisfaction and maturity. You will have exchanged immature behavior for relief of stress. You are also practicing to surrender. This is indeed "How It Works."

Given to thinking in grandiose terms, we are ready to surrender everything. We will quit smoking, lose weight, begin exercising, find a relationship, go back to school, and get a better job after 90 days of sobriety. Yes, your way. I'm surrendering. No. To attempt to give up all your bad habits at once is setting yourself up for failure. The load will look too great to tackle and sabotage will set in. If you feel that all of your habits are so important, maybe you are overestimating the importance of these things you do. Take small segments, one step at a time.

Traditionally, 12-step work is a critical component to successful recovery. This is good practice for surrender. Exchange a little time to help someone else. Volunteer in a detox program, answer the phone at Central, or work in a community activity. Think of this in terms of surrender and exchange. Don't be embarrassed to say, "I am doing this for selfish reasons. I need to surrender my will, my desires, my impulses, to help others, and thus learn more about how to surrender." Sound strange? Just try it.

From surrender comes the final peace. Letting go of the need to control opens our lives to endless possibilities. But we must surrender—give up the fight with ourselves and with the world around us to begin to enjoy our lives fully.

22

COPING WITH CHANGE

More recently than changing a diaper, I changed my whole life. How? Why? Very simply, I reached a point where I could no longer deny to myself (what friends and family had known for a longer time) that my life had become unmanageable. And, with a great deal of love and support, I changed that. Considering the resulting miracle of sobriety, why then do I resist more change today? Why do you?

Since the beginning of time, the universe has been in constant flux—changing. From the moment of conception, each of us is in constant motion—physically, emotionally, and socially changing. It is not too grandiose to say that the survival of the planet and all its creatures (including alcoholics) is dependent on the capacity to adjust, to accommodate, to mutate—to change.

Why then does the idea of change strike fear into most of our recovering hearts?

Physiological—our bodies automatically control much of our capacity to change. Most of us have heard terms like neutral pathways, muscle memory, neuron firing—phrases which are associated with the way animals and humans learn. Because the learning process alters physical structures in the brain over time—relearning or altering these structures also takes time.

Further, the survival instincts which protected primitive humans still protect us. If Nancy Neanderthal changed her mind and sampled every pretty, appetizing-looking fruit she encountered, she might eat poison. Her mind does not allow her to change what she has learned or been taught until some further evidence comes along—usually over time. (I still haven't learned this lesson where men are concerned. I go for the pretty outside. But, I digress . . .).

Emotionally, Freud and others tell us that much of our response to life is based on unconscious adjustment to control basic (and dangerous or frightening) impulses. Thus, on a date, a woman may allow a few drinks to reduce her conscious control, because subconsciously she is afraid to be sexual and flirtatious.

Socially, culturally, we learn that rewards and punishment are based on making the right choices. Change involves these rewards and punishments (both real and imagined). Have you ever evaluated a bad relationship with the rationalization, "If I give him up, I'll be alone?" To protect ourselves from pain and punishment, we often project a negative outcome from change.

The capacity to change, then, is the ability to re-learn, react, risk, repeat, refocus, and rebound. It involves physical reprogramming, insight into the emotional components, and clarity of values.

In *As Bill Sees It* there is no listing for the topic of change. But there are 44 references to growth, 10 references to progress, and 14 to open-mindedness, not to mention 15 references to willingness.

Change comes in many forms. Some broad categories encompass:

- External changes: Job transfers, eviction, terrorism, car trouble, poisoned grapes, dog bites, winning the lottery, chairs facing a different direction in an AA meeting.
- Emotional changes: Relationships ending, health, stress, aging, empty nests. Many, many emotional adjustments are required on a daily basis.
- Social changes: Changing roles of women and men, family structures, technology, occupational demands, new freedoms—opportunities abound.

With the potentially limitless list, what can any of us do to handle the stress of change?

Wonder how Ashton Kutcher does it? What's Eli Manning's secret? Not to mention Jennifer Lopez. In a study of Fortune 500 executives, researchers found two key factors: executives who handle stress well identify their secrets as, "See Change—Read Challenge." Recover quickly—let go.

Let's translate some of that to practical suggestions that might work for you. Adjusting takes time. You can speed up the process by:

- Acting "as if": Put the change or event in the future. Pretend it has already happened. Act "as if" you are a pound slimmer, in a good frame of mind, confident, and secure.
- Getting excited: Talk about the change as a challenge, a problem to be solved, and a puzzle that is fun.
- Taking a mini-break: To regain perspective and balance take a break. A weekend getaway is a great idea. If that's unrealistic, try breathing, a movie, a walk in the park, or on the beach. The idea is to break the negative cycle and refocus on the big picture. As my friend Lari often tells me, "It's only life—not brain surgery."

- Making a list: Making a list of only the positive in the change situation. Include positive outcomes, projections of good things coming from the change.

- Planning self-improvement: Examine what of your fear comes from real rather than imagined outcomes. Look at the need for improvement. Do you need more skill and can this be obtained in realistic ways—classes, tutors, etc.? Is this an opportunity to improve your personal image, communication skills, or public speaking techniques? There are many resources available that abound with services and professionals who can help. Free classes as well as low-cost consultations are readily available in any area of self-improvement.

- Coming from strength: Facing any sort of change, the positive as well as the negative, is better handled when the body and mind are on our side. Keeping in shape, eating and drinking in healthy patterns, getting lots of fresh air, and keeping healthy and happy cheerleaders around you is a definite must. Now is not the time to binge on sugar or pasta, overdo the caffeine, and toss and turn as you rehash your fears.

Change is inevitable—a fact of life. Life without change is death. Most of us who are recovering know the opposite of change. For too long our lives seemed not to change at all. The endless monotony of sameness was ensured by our drinking and using. Today, through sober living, there are many challenges. By knowing yourself, building a support network to see you through difficult times, and by developing new and workable coping skills, not only will change be manageable, but the promise of clean and sober living will come true.

BIBLIOGRAPHY

"About Migraine." American Migraine Foundation. http://www. americanmigrainefoundation.org/whatismigraine.aspx (accessed January 27, 2012).

"Abraham Maslow and the Biology of Human Values." Holistic Educator. www.holisticeducator.com/maslow.htm (accessed December 9, 2012).

"Alcohol and HIV/AIDS: Intertwining Stories." National Institute on Alcohol Abuse and Alcoholism. http://pubs.niaaa.nih.gov/ publications/AA80/AA80.htm (accessed January 28, 2012).

Alcoholics Anonymous World Services, Inc.. "The Twelve Steps Illustrated." Alcoholics Anonymous. www.aa.org/pdf/products/ p-55_twelvestepsillustrated.pdf (accessed January 15, 2013).

American Heritage Dictionary. "Love." 2011. Houghton Mifflin Harcourt.

"The Big Book Online." Alcoholics Anonymous. http://www.aa.org/ bigbookonline/en_tableofcnt.cfm (accessed December 10, 2012).

Buscaglia, Leo. "Love: What Life is All About . . . ." 2004. indwelt. http://www.indwelt.com/books/other/lblove.html (accessed January 16, 2013).

Cox, Lauren. "Managing Headaches Without Pain Medication— ABC News." ABC News. http://abcnews.go.com/Health/ PainManagement/managing-headaches-pain-medication/ story?id=10642271 (accessed January 16, 2013).

Fromm, Erich. The Art of Loving. 1956. Reprint, New York: Harper & Row, 2006.

Herald Sun (Melbourne), "Research finds many women need alcohol to enjoy sex," September 24, 2009, sec. The Other Side. http://www.heraldsun.com.au/news/the-other-side/research-finds-many-women-need-alcohol-to-enjoy-sex/story-e6frfhk6-1225778898667 (accessed January 28, 2012).

"HIV among Women." Centers for Disease Control and Prevention. http://www.cdc.gov/hiv/topics/women/index.htm (accessed September 1, 2012).

Hodge, Marshall Bryant. Your Fear of Love. Garden City: Doubleday, 1967.

Holmes, Thomas, and Richard Rahe. "Social Readjustment Rating Scale." University Counseling & Consulting Services. 2003. www.uccs.umn.edu/oldsite/lasc/handouts/socialreadjustment.html (accessed January 15, 2013).

Jampolsky, Gerald G.. "Love Is Letting Go Of Fear." 2010. Scribd. www.scribd.com/doc/92929189/Love-Is-Letting-Go-of-Fear-Third-Edition (accessed January 15, 2013).

Reece, Michael, Debby Herbenick, J. Dennis Fortenberry, Stephanie Sanders, Vanessa Schick, Brian Dodge, and Susan Middlestaldt. "National Survey of Sexual Health and Behavior." 2010. Indiana University. http://www.nationalsexstudy.indiana.edu (accessed January 16, 2013).

University of Illinois at Urbana-Champaign. "What You Should Know About Sex & Alcohol." McKinley Health Center. http://www.mckinley.illinois.edu/handouts/sex_alcohol.html (accessed January 29, 2012).

Vogels, Josey. "Women Have Lots of Casual Sex--Get Over It." Alternet. http://www.alternet.org/story/146631/women_have_lots_of_casual_sex_--_get_over_it (accessed January 16, 2013).

W., Bill. "As Bill Sees It: The A.A. Way of Life." 1967. Alcoholics Anonymous World Services Inc.

"Women & Alcohol: The Hidden Risks of Drinking." HelpGuide. http://www.helpguide.org/harvard/women_alcohol.htm (accessed January 16, 2012).